Interrogating Development

Interrogating Development

State, Displacement and Popular Resistance in North East India

MONIRUL HUSSAIN

SAGE Studies on India's North East

SAGE Los Angeles • London • New Delhi • Singapore
www.sagepublications.com

First published in 2008 by

 SAGE Publications India Pvt Ltd
B1/I-1 Mohan Cooperative Industrial Area
Mathura Road
New Delhi 110 044, India
www.sagepub.in

SAGE Publications Inc
2455 Teller Road
Thousand Oaks, California 91320, USA

SAGE Publications Ltd
1 Oliver's Yard, 55 City Road
London EC1Y 1SP, United Kingdom

SAGE Publications Asia-Pacific Pte Ltd
33 Pekin Street
#02-01 Far East Square
Singapore 048763

Published by Vivek Mehra for SAGE Publications India Pvt Ltd, typeset in 10.5/13pt Aldine401 BT by Star Compugraphics Private Limited, Delhi and printed at Chaman Enterprises, New Delhi.

Library of Congress Cataloging-in-Publication Data

Hussain, Monirul, 1952–
  Interrogating development : state, displacement and popular resistance in North East India / Monirul Hussain.
    p. cm.—
  Includes bibliographical references and index.
    1. Internally displaced persons—India—Assam—Social conditions. 2. Ethnic conflict—India—Assam. 3. Assam (India)—Social conditions. 4. India, Northeastern—Ethnic relations.   I. Title. II. State.
HV640.4.I4H86   362.87—dc22   2007   2007035240

ISBN: 978-0-7619-3575-9 (Pb)   978-81-7829-736-1 (India-Pb)

SAGE Team: Sugata Ghosh, Janaki Srinivasan

This book is dedicated to some of the wonderful women of India:

Medha Patkar

Mahasweta Devi

Aruna Roy

Brinda Karat

Nandita Haksar

Shabana Azmi

Arundhati Roy

Teesta Setalvad

Sunita Narain

and

those countless women and men

who are fighting for people's right

as part of a larger struggle for substantive

democracy and secularism in India.

Contents

List of Tables

Table

Figure

List of Abbreviations

ABEF	All Bodo Employees' Federation
ABSU	All Bodo Students' Union
ADB	Asian Development Bank
AGP	*Asom Gana Parishad*
ARSU	All Rabha Students' Union
ATDCC	Anti-Tamanthi Dam Campaign Committee
BDLD	Bodoland Demand Legislative Party
BHEL	Bharat Heavy Electricals Limited
BTAD	Bodoland Territorial Autonomous District
BTC	Bodoland Territorial Council
CATD	Committee Against Tipaimukh Dam
CCDD	Citizens Concern for Dams and Development
CEA	Central Electricity Authority
CHT	Chittagong Hill Tracts
CPM	Cachar Paper Mills
CPR	Common Property Resource
DHP	Dumbur Hydroelectric Project
DIR	Defence of India Rule
DONER	Development of North East Region
DPs	Displaced Persons
GAIL	Gas Authority of India Limited
IBA	Important Bird Area
IDP	Internally Displaced Persons
IMF	International Monetary Fund
LAQ 1894	Land Acquisition Act 1894
LSP	Lower Subansiri Project
MNF	Mizo National Front
MPCB	Mizoram Pollution Control Board
NBA	*Narmada Bachao Andolan*
NDA	National Democratic Alliance

NEEPCO	North Eastern Electric Power Corporation
NEFA	North East Frontier Agency
NHPC	National Hydroelectric Power Corporation
NHRC	National Human Rights Commission
NPM	Nagaon Paper Mills
NSM	New Social Movements
OIL	Oil India Limited
ONGC	Oil and Natural Gas Corporation Limited
PAPs	Project-Affected Persons
PDP	Pagladiya Dam Project
PMSV	People's Movement for Subansiri Valley
SVBC	*Siang Valley Bachao Committee*
TMP	Tipaimukh Multi-purpose Project
TVS	Tale Valley Sanctuary
WCD	World Commission on Dams

Acknowledgements

This study is an outcome of South Asia Regional Fellowship (Senior) awarded to me by the Social Science Research Council (SSRC) of New York in 2004. As part of the Fellowship, I was attached to the OKD Institute of Social Change and Development (OKDISCD), Guwahati, from April to July 2004. First and foremost, I must thank the SSRC (New York) for selecting me for the prestigious fellowship, OKDISCD for granting me the affiliation, and the Gauhati University for granting me necessary leave to avail the fellowship and devote three months completely to the project.

Besides these three institutions, I am also personally indebted to Dr Itty Abraham and Ms Malini Sur of the SSRC (New York), Prof. A.N.S. Ahmed, the Director of the OKDISCD, and Dr G.N. Talukdar, Vice Chancellor, Gauhati University, for their help and encouragement at different stages of the project. I am also greatly obliged to Dr Ranabir Samaddar of the Calcutta Research Group, Kolkata, and Prof. B.S. Chimni, Vice Chancellor of the West Bengal National University of Juridical Sciences, Kolkata and Prof. Imtiaz Ahmad of Jawaharlal Nehru University, New Delhi, for their critical comments on the draft proposal of this study.

I am especially grateful to a well-known scholar on development-induced displacement in India, Dr Walter Fernandes, Director of the North Eastern Social Research Centre (NESRC), Guwahati. I have used some fresh data from the field in the third chapter of this study from an ongoing and of course, a much larger research project undertaken by the NESRC. I am grateful to Dr Fernandes who kindly agreed for a partnership in data collection and data sharing. Besides, Ms Gita Bharali, Research Associate of the NESRC helped me immensely in systematically arranging the database for this study.

Ms Saba Hussain, currently of Greenpeace, Bangalore and Ms Barnalee Choudhury, an ICSSR Doctoral Fellow at the Department of Political Science, Gauhati University have offered me all the necessary research assistance from the beginning till the end of the project. Ms Sanghamitra Nath and Ms Gulshan Parveen provided editorial assistance. Mirza Mohammed Irshad and Subhas Barman, Research Scholars in the Department of Political Science, Gauhati University, accompanied me in my field work. They shared with me all the pain and pleasure of field investigation. I am thankful to them. It is a pleasure to have such wonderful students. Meeting and interacting with the 'threatened people' who have been struggling to resist the brutality of development through sustained collective mobilization was a great learning experience for me. I am greatly indebted to them. During our field visit they had given us enough time, love, affection and care.

I also must thank my esteemed colleagues and students at the Centre for the Study of Social Systems, School of Social Sciences, Jawaharlal Nehru University, New Delhi for their comments on the seminar presentation I made during my brief tenure as Visiting Professor there during July–August 2005. Prof. Dulal C. Goswami and Prof. Sandhya Goswami of Gauhati University helped me immensely in completing this project. I am also grateful to my esteemed colleagues at the Department of Political Science, Gauhati University; Prof. Niru Hazarika, Dr Alaka Sarma, Dr Noni Gopal Mahanta, Dr Akhil Ranjan Dutta, Dr Dhruba Pratim Sarma and Mr Subharajit Konwar for their interest in my work.

Along with Itty in Washington D.C. and Malini in Kolkata, my wife, Runima, and our children, Farhan and Sabreena, here in Guwahati had to bear with my prolonged engagement with the project beyond the stipulated time frame. I deeply appreciate their patience.

Lastly, I must express my gratitude to Dr Sugata Ghosh and SAGE India for their keen interest in my project and decision to publish the same.

Monirul Hussain
Department of Political Science
Gauhati University

1

Introduction

Though economic development brings about qualitative changes and stability in political and economic lives of various communities, it is now a well-accepted fact that it also simultaneously degrades the socio-economic and cultural lives of many marginalized social groups of the same society. It is important to recognize that the contemporary development process has its beneficiaries as well as victims. India's post-colonial experience of state-sponsored development projects unmistakably signals that the benefits of such projects have been usurped largely by the economically and politically dominant sections of society. Development has been biased and unequal in its manifestations. In many cases, it has been brutal, ruthless and inhuman in its consequences. At certain levels, criminalization of development has also taken place wherein politicians, bureaucrats, technocrats and mafias masquerading as contractors and social workers have collectively siphoned off the fund meant for development.

Development has its own network of vested interests and in many cases the state too has condoned them. This exercise proposes to stress on this aspect of development that has degraded the socio-economic, cultural and political lives of several groups of marginalized ethnic communities. Unbalanced economic development has obviously contributed towards unbalancing human lives and community structure. In order to understand this underrated and largely ignored aspect, we have confined ourselves specifically to locate the development-induced displacement of population. Obviously, this displacement is imposed, forced and involuntary in nature despite occurring within a democratic political system. Well-known jurist V.R. Krishna Iyer made this pertinent observation:

> India today is the victim of development. Ask Medha Patkar or Sundarlal Bahuguna about the victims of development ... the perilous process of environmental injuries, the polluted rivers, the disappearing mountains, the depleting mineral resources, the uprooted tribal, the submerged mother earth, and the vast multitude of marginalized human beings who are appalled by the terrorism of development and await their turn to be sacrificed at the inexorably market hungry, altar of poignant, irrevocable 'blood and iron' Development Maniacs (Iyer 1998).

Vandergeest observes rightly that development in its forms is inherently a spatial activity. Since development is fundamentally about reorganizing space, all development has the potential of causing displacement (Vandergeest 2003: 47). It has been estimated that infrastructural development programmes displace 10 million people every year in developing countries.

> It has been observed that the development operations have not only grown considerably but have also been handled disastrously, generating unprecedented resistance and high international visibility, for example, the Narmada Dams in India. Population densities keep on increasing, and every new major infrastructural programme requires 'space' that is often inhabited or already otherwise used. Displacement is not just an economic transition, substituting property with monetary compensation; it also involves 'resettlement' and requires true 'rehabilitation' (Desai and Potter 2002: 426).

Like many other developing countries of Asia and Africa, India too generated a massive army of different categories of Internally Displaced Persons (henceforth IDPs) during the post-colonial period. Development projects are one of the many causes of people's displacement. It is little known that India has one of the highest rates of development-induced displacement. The consequence of the state choosing areas to launch development projects time and again, has led to a high proportion of tribals falling in the category of IDPs. Moreover, the state addressing its powerful vested interest is least concerned about tribal lives and livelihood. During the last 50 years, some 3,300 big dams have been built in India (NRC 2002). Most of them have led to large-scale forced eviction of vulnerable groups. The situation of tribal people is of special concern, as they constitute 40 to 50 per cent of the total displaced population. However, there are no reliable official statistics on the number of people displaced by development projects. Official figures state that as many as 21 to 33 million persons are likely to have been displaced (Fernandes 2000). But the database studies show the numbers to be as high as 50 million. Case studies indicate that most official figures are underestimates, for example, by official count 1,10,000 persons were displaced by the Hirakud dam in Orissa, while research estimates put them at 1,80,000 (Pattanaik, Das and Mishra 1987). The Farakka Super Thermal Plant in West Bengal has officially affected none, but the World Bank (1994) speaks of 63,325 IDPs after this project. Many more such cases can be cited.

It is significant that tribals or *adivasis* constitute more than half of the development-induced displaced persons (DPs) in India. According to the Commissioner for Scheduled Castes and Scheduled Tribes, they account for about 60 per cent of total project-induced displaced persons. A reason for the high proportion of tribals among IDPs is that the number of projects in their areas has been growing since the 1970s. For example, of the 117 dams above 50 metre height either completed or underway in 1990, 40 were in tribal areas. This has happened despite India being a signatory to the Elimination of Racial Discrimination protocol!

Here, in this exercise, we are trying to find the linkage between state-sponsored development projects and its consequent displacement of population in the specific context of a 'non-mainstream' region of India, that is, North East India in general and the state of Assam in particular. We conceptualize Assam, or for that matter the entire North East India, as a periphery of India, which is again a periphery within the larger global context. It is posited at the bottom of the hierarchy of peripheries. North East suffers from being both, far from the centre and decisively dependent on it. This strategically important region is surrounded by four countries—China, Myanmar, Bhutan and Bangladesh—and is connected with the rest of India through a narrow corridor and a precarious communication network incapable of meeting popular aspirations for rapid economic development of the region. North East India is the home of innumerable nationalities, national minorities and ethnic groups belonging to different races, colours, religious persuasions and linguistic groups; all standing at visibly uneven levels of socio-economic development. A very similar unevenness is also apparent in terms of their integration and identification with the pan-Indian nationalism and the Indian nation-state (see Baruah 2000 and 2005, Guha 1980, Hussain 1990, 1993, 2005a, Misra 2000, Nag 2002, etc.). Needless to say, North East is one of the poorly governed regions of India (Hussain 2003). In the post-colonial period it remained a politically sensitive, violent and disturbed region, of course with periodic lulls. The region also experienced massive environmental degradation. The great earthquake of 1950 devastated the region, particularly the northern bank of the Bramhaputra valley in Upper Assam. Change of the courses of innumerable rivers and streams, perennial flood and massive river bank erosion in the valleys, unprecedented deforestation, landslide in the hills and other natural and human made disasters have affected the people and ecology of the region very severely. In such a complex situation, the question of development emerged as a very crucial issue for the region. Like the rest of the country, the people of the North East too started perceiving the post-colonial state as an institution of development 'giver'. Following independence, like other decolonized societies of the South, the popular expectation was very high for development of the region from the post-colonial state.

Here, we are mainly concerned with state-sponsored development projects and activities. Private investment in development projects in this part of India is abysmally low. Hence, we confine ourselves to development projects taken up by the state. Such projects seem to contribute significantly towards the economic development of the region without applying a compass of responsibility, equity, ethics and justice. Development projects suffered severely because of their lack of concern for people and environment. Many such projects have displaced a large number of people, mostly living at the margins of the society. They have been perniciously injurious to the ecology of the North East.

This study is an effort to enable one to comprehend this seemingly brutal aspect of development; besides understanding the nature, direction and quality of social change in North East India as a part of India's post-colonial project of modernity and nation-building. In other words, I am attempting to understand the ongoing encounter between the development giver and a large section of development taker in a situation of dialogic vacuum.

In the face of rising expectation among the masses following independence, the incipient post-colonial Indian state became active in the socio-economic development process as a part of its larger nation-building project. State-sponsored development projects became a major issue for the government and the people. It became much more crucial for a frontier region like North East, particularly Assam, entrapped as it was in a high degree of economic exploitation, extraction and marginalization as a colonial hinterland. The people of the region expected development to bring about significant improvement in their living condition. They expected their well-being to be the essence of development during the post-colonial period.

We must also point out unambiguously that the post-colonial Indian state embarked upon the development process without restructuring the bureaucracy that it inherited from the colonial state. Development continued to be top-down and a highly centralized process that virtually excluded popular participation. On the other hand, notwithstanding the emergence of a strong public sector during the first four decades of independence and its closer ties with the erstwhile Soviet Union and the Socialist Block, India has fundamentally remained on the capitalist path of development. India's quest for modernization remained within the broad framework of capitalist development, and all distortions of uneven and capitalist development manifested themselves very prominently in the North Eastern region and on the people living therein.

Before entering into the substantive theme, we must point out explicitly the meaning of IDP. The United Nations Guiding Principles on Internal Displacement defines:

> Internally displaced persons are persons or groups of persons who have been forced or obliged to flee or leave their homes or place of habitual residence, in particular as a result of, or in order to, avoid the effects of armed conflict, situation of generalized violence, violation of human rights or natural or human made disasters, and who have not crossed an internationally recognized state border (UN 1999: 1, Kalin 2000: 1).

From the above definition, we can broadly categorize three types of IDPs (a) conflict-induced, (b) natural disaster, environment induced, and (c) human made or development-induced IDPs. Needless to say, in some cases all these categories overlap with one another. They are involuntarily ejected from their homes and land, and very often forced to live in relief camps. Hence, they find themselves in situations very similar to that of the refugees. But they are not treated as refugees, as unlike refugees they have not crossed any international border. Therefore, they are not entitled to the protection guaranteed by the international community to the refugees. Besides, many nation-states cannot provide them protection. On the other hand, some countries are unwilling to seek international help and protection because that affects their 'prestige' as a nation-state and their 'sovereignty'. In many cases, sovereignty becomes a wall against care and protection of the IDPs. Hence, in the absence of an international as well as domestic protection regime, the plight of the IDPs can sometimes be more precarious than that of the refugees. We should add here that India has neither signed nor ratified the United Nations Convention on Refugees of 1951, or the Protocol of 1967. Hence, at the 'official/legal' level India is not committed to provide protection to the refugees. However, this does not deter India from protecting refugees and IDPs. Notwithstanding the absence of the word IDP in the Indian constitution, the very spirit of the constitution obviously protects all the citizens of the country including the IDPs.

One must note that since the end of the Cold War, while the number of refugees has shown a gradual decline, the number of IDPs has seen a manifold increase globally. Hence, along with the concern for refugees, concern for IDPs too has been expressed repeatedly by the international humanitarian community as both of them are highly vulnerable and excluded groups. Like refugees, Roberta Cohen observed succinctly:

> IDPs are generally in desperate straits. Because they are forcibly separated from their homes, communities and livelihoods, they become more vulnerable to starvation and diseases than others in the population and they are easy targets for physical assault, forced recruitment and sexual abuse. Indeed, the highest malnutrition rates recorded in emergencies in recent years have been in populations of internally displaced persons and the highest mortality rates ever recorded have involved IDPs (Cohen 2003: 20–21).

Objectives of Study

This study is an endeavour to comprehend the complex relationship between state-sponsored development projects and the consequent massive displacement of population in North East India in general, and Assam in particular. In the absence of a detailed study till now, this study is likely to be the first of its kind to attempt at understanding the problem in a detailed manner. However, a much larger database study has just been completed and is presently awaiting publication (Fernandes and Bharali 2006). This study has dealt with development-induced displacement and deprivation in the state of Assam both in quantitative and qualitative terms (ibid.).

In our study, we are attempting to prepare a dossier of development-induced displacement of population in Assam even though incomplete. The study aims at understanding the response of people who are facing the threat of displacement as a consequence of the commissioning of mega dam projects in North East India. Our study endeavours more at interrogating post-colonial development processes, raising questions and situating people at the centre of the research rather than providing solutions. In order to do that, we have made an attempt to understand the popular resistance to the brutality of development. In other words, this study attempts at locating the relationship between the state as a development giver and the people as the development taker.

A significant number of people have gradually refused to become silent sufferers of the ill effects of development and are now raising their voices collectively to counter development plans that they feel go against their interest and existence. In the process, they are profoundly influencing the emergence of an alternative development paradigm for India and the North East.

Database

This project uses existing data on the issues involved from both primary and secondary sources. Besides, we have also tried to generate some data on the basis of field experience. We have also used some fresh data from a recently completed project of North Eastern Social Research Centre, Guwahati under the guidance of Walter Fernandes, well-known scholar of development-induced displacement in India, who agreed for a partnership in data collection and sharing. We have used this data very extensively in the third chapter while presenting and analyzing the quantum of land acquisition and its resultant displacement of population in Assam. Nevertheless, we believe that whatever empirical data we have presented in this project unmistakably points to the enormity of the problem of land acquisition for state-sponsored development projects and the consequent massive displacement of people in the regions already specified.

Method of Data Collection

The data used in Chapter Three has been collected from official sources—the district administration and gazettes of the state government—that is, the government of Assam. The government is the main source of the data on land acquisition, compensation and displacement. However, since this valuable data has been kept in absolute disorder, it was an arduous task organizing them into a presentable tabular form. We must also specify that we have used the category Not Available (NA) while classifying the data decade-wise for land acquisition and displacement, where adequate data were unavailable. Our field investigators found some old data without dates which have been put under the NA category. Nevertheless, the collected data unmistakably points to the enormity of the problem of land acquisition for development purposes and its consequent displacement of population.

The quantum of land acquisition and displacement is perhaps much larger than what this study has been able to provide in terms of official data, as disorganized documentation makes for a monumental obstacle in assessing the extent of the problem. It is very important for the government to have a proper database on land acquisition and displacement, as there are numerous instances of contradictory data being available from various departments of the same government. The lack of reliable data, in many situations, forced us to resort to extrapolation of data by adding other reliable sources. In the land acquisition data, all area is in acres unless otherwise mentioned as being in hectares or *bighas*.

While analyzing the popular resistance to mega dam projects, we have depended on both media reports and our field observation. Our interaction and dialogue with the threatened people have immensely enhanced our understanding of the development paradigm of the Indian state and have provided more insights than what hard official data could do.

Structure of Study

This study consists of five interrelated chapters. The first chapter introduces the study, its objective, database and methods. The second chapter is an attempt at making a general dossier of development-induced displacement of population in the North East. It is fundamentally an overview of the situation. The third chapter attempts to understand the displacement situation quantitatively, as far as possible, using empirical data from the field. It is an endeavour to understand the situation in the state of Assam more specifically using both official and unofficial data. The fourth chapter is an effort at understanding the response of people towards development, in the specific context of the ongoing construction of mega dams throughout the North East. Here, we would particularly like to look into the emerging popular resistance movements against some development projects in the pipeline.

Why do some people want development and dams and some do not? Some people are very optimistic about state-sponsored development projects while some are very deeply pessimistic about them. The latter perceive development as the source of frustration, alienation and estrangement from their own state and society. The state is also seen as an aggressor that transgresses into their life, shelter, livelihood, human rights and dignity.

The fifth chapter draws certain broad conclusions and explores policy implications on the basis of the preceding chapters. Is there an alternative to the brutality of development? Is there a humane alternative which respects the voice of the people, their legitimate rights, aspirations and frustrations, individual as well as collective identity and dignity? Can we eradicate developmental brutality and replace it with a more humane paradigm that protects the marginalized—their land, shelter and livelihood—and enhances their capabilities? Instead of disempowering, can development empower the marginalized? Can moral and ethical dimensions form a part of the development discourse? Can we ignore the ecological issues and concerns of development projects? Should the Indian state implement the same development discourse that is being enforced in the rest of the country, to a peripheral region like the North East with its own diverse specificities? Does development need to respect the historical specificities of the people and the region? Is it not possible to develop an alternative development paradigm that takes care of popular aspirations involving their distinct community, polity, economy and culture?

2

Imposing Development

Introducing the Incomplete Dossier of Displacement

> ... the livelihood and unique culture of the tribal should be protected when development projects are undertaken in areas inhabited by them.
>
> —*K.R. Narayanan, President of India*

North East India, particularly the plains of Assam, received a large number of migrants from the rest of India during the colonial period under the direct patronage of the colonial state (Hussain 1993, 1999, 2000, 2002, 2005A, 2005B, 2006A, 2006B, 2007). At that time, because of abundance of land and low density of population, it was possible to accommodate a large number of migrants in Assam. Needless to say, except a small, middle and entrepreneurial class, the huge majority of these migrants were the marginalized people of East Bengal, the Chotanagpur region, Nepal and such other places. We need to emphasize that most of these migrants, particularly those who came from East Bengal and the Chotanagpur region, were in fact displaced by the political economy of colonialism. Hence, during the colonial period, we find the North East/Assam playing host to a large number of displaced and uprooted people from the rest of the country. This situation saw a gradual change in the post-colonial phase. The status of the region transformed from being that of a host to a generator of a very large number of conflict-, environment- and development-induced displacement of population during the post-colonial period. Though massive internal displacement of population is continuing unabated due to various reasons, in this project we are confining ourselves to the study of development-induced displacement of people in North East India.

We have already noted the path of development that the Indian state has chosen for its post-colonial nation-building project. Despite adopting the capitalist path, the Indian State was well aware of its role in the face of popular expectation generated by the anti-colonial struggle and attainment of freedom. The state kept certain areas of development as its own responsibility as a part of the Nehruvian vision of India. In addition to certain conventional areas like internal and external security, health and education, the state engaged itself in building the socio-economic infrastructure; communication, railways, aviation, road transport and power, and various areas of industry like steel, oil, paper, etc.

For an underdeveloped region like the North East, the engagement of the state was very crucial for developing the infrastructure and industries. The state required a huge amount of land for the development process. Most of the land was either privately owned by individuals or collectively owned as Common Property Resource (CPR). In the absence of industry, most people were engaged in agriculture, and thus arable land was not only an asset, but also the means of their survival and livelihood. Since the state needed more land than was directly under its ownership, it acquired land from the common people in its developmental pursuits. The commonly accepted notion of the Indian state as a development giver, enhanced the legitimacy of the state in acquiring land from the people in 'Public Interest'. In the process, the state became the patron and the citizens became the clients for a long period of time after independence. Emergence of this patron–client relationship virtually barred the process of development with dignity (see Bhaduri 2006). In a democracy like India, according to Bhaduri, 'the patron–client relation between the state and its citizens is not desirable, perhaps not even viable in the long run' (ibid.: 39). The public had to involuntarily surrender a large part of their land to the state at a price far below the market rate, and many had to give their land free of cost for the development of the country. The legacy of the all-powerful colonial coercive state apparatus continued unabated against the poor and the marginalized people even during the post-colonial period. Consequently, the development process initiated by the state induced a massive displacement of population. In the absence of any tangible policy of resettlement and rehabilitation, the state forced the displaced people into a situation of impoverishment and further marginalization. The issue of displacement has made development an issue of rights and dignity.

To begin with, here we are exploring certain areas which induced displacement of population in Assam during the post-colonial period. We need to note here that present day Nagaland was a district of Assam till 1963. Similarly, both Meghalaya and Mizoram were parts of Assam till the reorganization of Assam in 1972. Hence, in this chapter we have also included them. Besides, we are also examining briefly a few other development projects that led to the displacement of population in Tripura and Arunachal Pradesh.

Security

We have already stated the geo-strategic location of North East India. This region is surrounded by China, Bangladesh, Bhutan and Myanmar. The region suffers from an alienation from mainland India due to certain historical and geographical reasons. The North East is connected physically with the rest of India through a narrow corridor. As a part of its security threat perception and defence requirement, the post-colonial Indian state established new camps and cantonments to station the armed forces in various parts of the region in addition to those established by the colonial state in the wake of Second World War. It led to a higher concentration of armed forces in North East India during the post-colonial period. It would be important to recollect here that North East India was directly involved in two crucial wars that independent India fought—one against China in 1962 and the other against Pakistan in 1971. The 1971 war was the last big war that India fought from the North East against external forces. Additionally, the Indian Army and a large number of paramilitary forces have been engaged in fighting innumerable 'small wars' internally in the North East against various indigenous insurgent groups struggling for 'illusive' independence beginning with the Naga rebellion as India gained Independence. As a result of such political developments and 'state-centric security' requirements; the state acquired land for defence and security purposes. Consequently, a very large number of ordinary citizens were displaced by the state. In most cases, it was the marginalized groups that had to sacrifice immensely for both external and internal security of post-colonial India.

Besides land acquisition, the regrouping of villages by the Indian armed forces in the wake of the Mizo rebellion in the mid-sixties under the draconian Defence of India Rule (DIR) 1957 led to massive displacement of tribal population in the erstwhile Lushai Hill District of Assam. In order to contain the Mizo rebellion led by the Mizo National Front (MNF), the Indian Army severely dislocated the Mizo tribal economy and the community structure. The idea behind regrouping of villages, Subir Bhaumik observes:

> … was to keep the rebels away from the sources of food, but it also removed the farmers to roadside and semi-urban locations from where it was impossible to cultivate their fields. The whole population became dependent on Indian public distribution system and remains so till date (Bhaumik 2000: 142).

It has been estimated that about 45,000 tribal people from 109 scattered villages were grouped into 18 group centres (Lianzela 2002: 247). This measure was taken at a time when the population of the district was less than 3 lakhs (Census of India 1961). The displacement ratio, that is, 45,000 people out of a total of about 3 lakhs is undoubtedly a huge number. Regrouping of villages severely affected the community life of the Mizos. After the completion of the first two phases, the armed forces wanted to go in for the third phase mostly in the Southern Mizo hills; however, the Gauhati High Court stayed this operation and rescued the rest of the population from regrouping/displacement.

Power Sector

Soon after independence, particularly Assam and Tripura had to engage in rehabilitating a large number of Hindu Bengali refugees from East Pakistan for a long time. Because of the lack of adequate infrastructure for economic development, the post-colonial state was engaged initially in gradually building the infrastructure. For example, the first bridge over the river Brahmaputra came up as late as in 1963. One can see the advent of some state-sponsored development projects only in early sixties and late seventies of the last century. The Assam State Electricity Board, an autonomous body under the State Government of Assam, took up the Umium Hydroelectric Project at Barapani about 16 kilometres away from Shillong, the then state capital of Assam in early sixties. The construction of a large artificial lake submerged a large tract of land and displaced a large number of Khasi tribals from their ancestral land. Again, establishment of three other thermal power plants under the Assam State Electricity Board, namely, Chandrapur Thermal Power Station (CTPS) at Chandrapur, Namrup Thermal Power Station (NTPS) at Namrup and Bongaigaon Thermal Power Station (BTPS) at Bongaigaon displaced several thousand people, mostly tribal. All these projects aiming at generating power affected the powerless tribals of both the hills and the plains of Assam severely. Now both CTPS and BTPS have become redundant and no longer produce any electricity and occupy large tracts of land meant to be utilized for public purposes, that is, to generate power. The NTPS too is in a very bad state, and is now producing only one-tenth power of its stipulated capacity. These are not only instances of misuse of public money and land, but all these power projects have also dishonoured the sacrifice made by the people.

Power sector reform under the neo-liberal paradigm has constricted the role of the state electricity boards. It has neither enhanced efficiency nor reduced corruption. They are now virtually forced to become buyers and sellers of power, not the generators. The responsibility of power generation has gone to the public sector undertakings under the Government of India and other big private parties. Now the Government of Assam is transferring its redundant plants to these bodies. An MoU was signed between the Government of Assam and the National Thermal Power Corporation (NTPC) on 30th May 2007 wherein the entire property and land of the BTPS was sold to NTPC at a nominal price of Re 1/only! This includes 2,300 *bigha*s of land which the state government acquired for the Assam State Electricity Board (see Our Special Correspondent 2007 and *Asamiya Pratidin* 2007). Perhaps, the other remaining redundant plants of the state electricity board will face a similar fate in the near future. It is difficult to get the exact data on land acquisition for the power sector in Assam. However, we have found that the government acquired huge tracts of tribal land, that is, approximately 7015.60 acres for the Kopili Hydroelectric Project. This plant has also not been able to meet its stipulated targets of power generation. Locals claim that this project failed because it was aimed only at raising the potential for power generation and not irrigation even though it was located near a perennially drought-prone area. The people of Nagaon and Morigaon districts allege that the devastating flood of 2004 that affected these two districts severely was the result of panic discharge of water from the water reservoir of the Kopili Hydroelectric Project during the high monsoon period. In popular perception, the dam and its operator, the North Eastern Electric Power Corporation (NEEPCO) were causing tremendous harm by releasing water at a time when all rivers were in spate during high monsoon. Needless to say, flood and river bank erosion displace a large number of people in Assam every year, and the Kopili Project is abetting this process. It would be worthwhile to recollect here that besides the Kopili Project, the bursting of Kuriechu dam in neighbouring Bhutan in 2004 had induced a devastating and prolonged flood in the adjacent Nalbari, Barpeta, Bongaigaon and southern parts of Kamrup districts in Lower Assam.

The development of the power sector in Tripura also led to a massive forced displacement of tribal population. The Dumbur Hydroelectric Project (DHP) displaced an estimated 8,000 tribal families and approximately 40,000 people from the project site. For a small state like Tripura, 40,000 people is a huge number. Among the various power projects, the DHP displaced the highest number of people. The state did not give adequate attention to the problem of resettlement and rehabilitation of the displaced population. The perpetual tribal insurgency also has its roots among the displaced people.

The North Eastern state of Tripura had to accept a maximum burden of partition-induced Hindu Bengali refugees, and this affected the indigenous tribal community very severely. In such a situation, it was a historic blunder to go in for the DHP for which a large tract of prime agricultural land was acquired from the indigenous tribal. This induced severe land and political alienation of the tribals from the state. Besides, the DHP failed to generate the targeted amount of power. It is increasingly becoming a non-viable project and a burden on the state of Tripura. Hence, there have been demands to decommission the project and alternatively to go in for a more viable gas based power project in Tripura (Bhaumik 2005: 201–4).

Presently the condition of the DHP is pathetic. A BBC East India correspondent on 3rd April 2007 reported that hundreds of indigenous tribes in Tripura flocked to reclaim the lands emerging from the dam's reservoir after a sharp drop in the water level there. The Tripura Police chased them away from the waterless reservoir (Bhaumik 2007). The Communist Party of India (Marxist) led government says it will not let anybody settle down on the lands emerging from the reservoir and has admitted that power generation has completely stopped since mid March 2007 (ibid.). Needless to say, this has happened because of the siltation and its consequent rise in the bed of the reservoir. Many tribals feel that the land should be reclaimed and systematically redistributed among 25,000 landless marginalized tribal peasants in the state to undo a historical injustice (ibid.). The DHP commissioned in 1974 has now virtually become redundant. A similar fate awaits few other reservoirs. It needs to be pointed out that all the existing seven hydroelectric projects in North East India have not been performing well. They generate only 319 MW against the installed capacity of 875 MW (ibid.). All this reflects the efficacy of the reservoir-based hydroelectric projects!

Besides, both Tripura and Arunachal Pradesh, the then North East Frontier Agency (NEFA), had to bear the brunt of the Kaptai Dam constructed on the Karnaphuli river across the international border in the Chittagong Hill Tracts (CHT) in erstwhile East Pakistan. This ambitious mega power project of the then East Pakistan government forcibly displaced a large number of Chakma and Hajong tribals. These two communities formed a religious and ethnic minority in East Pakistan, now Bangladesh. A large number of people ousted from the Kaptai Dam site entered India as refugees and settled down in Tripura and Arunachal Pradesh. Those who were resettled in Arunachal Pradesh under the sponsorship of the Government of India are now facing a serious threat to their existence as a result of sharpening of the Arunachali identity. Despite living in the state for the last four decades, they still remain a 'stateless community' waiting endlessly for an elusive citizenship. The stateless population in Arunachal Pradesh is now nearly 1,00,000. Here, one can see how the development-induced displaced people experience a threat of political conflict-induced displacement. Besides, the Chakma issue in Arunachal Pradesh has shown very pertinently that a development-induced displacement in one country may have significant spillover effects in another country; the way the DPs of the erstwhile East Pakistan became refugees and later stateless persons without citizenship rights in India.

Oil Sector

Assam is known for two major industries, tea and petroleum/oil since the colonial days. The first oil refinery of India was established at Digboi in Upper Assam in the late 19th century. During the post-colonial era, the state was involved greatly in the expansion of oil industry in India. Though there were highly organized protests against pumping of Assam's crude oil out of the state to feed a big refinery in Bihar, the oil industry in Assam developed significantly during the post-colonial period under the direct sponsorship of the state. New oil townships emerged at Duliajan, Noonmati, Narangi, Nazira, Bongaigaon and Numaligarh, in addition to the over a century old township of Digboi. In order to build these townships as a part of development projects, the state had to displace a large number of rural masses from their ancestral land. Some of these displaced people received compensation in cash and a very few could manage to get jobs at the lowest rank in these industries. The oil industry did not benefit the displaced. What the state did was far from being adequate. No state measures were taken to rehabilitate them properly. They were left to rehabilitate themselves and they remained the invisible oustees of development.

It is difficult to find the exact amount of land acquisition for the oil sector in Assam. Whatever land acquisition data we could collect from the official sources and are presenting here provides only a part of the whole story. For establishing the Bongaigaon Petrochemical Complex Limited popularly known as BRPL, the state government acquired 565 acres of private land and 5,435 acres Common Property Resource (CPR) land totalling to a massive 6,000 acres of land. Somewhat similar is the case of the Numaligarh Refinery Limited popularly known as NRL in Golaghat district. The Government of Assam acquired at least 269 acres of private land and 481 acres of CPR land totalling to 750 acres for the NRL (Baruah 1999: 20). Similar is the case of Noonmati Refinery located in Guwahati. The Government of Assam acquired 603 acres of private land and 3,397 acres of CPR land totalling to a massive 4,000 acres of land for the Noonmati Refinery. Cash compensation was given to the legal owners of the land. All the land occupants were not the legal owners, *pattadars*. Hence, only the state-recognized legal owners got the compensation. Consequently, a large number of DPs did not get any compensation. However, the larger chunk of newly acquired land belonged to the CPR category. Hence, acquisition of CPR land directly affected the livelihood and sustenance of a large number of Project-Affected Persons (PAPs), most of them, obviously tribal. The land acquired for the Noonmati Refinery in Guwahati belonged to the powerful non-tribal Assamese elites but in most cases the actual occupants were tribal. Establishment of Noonmati Refinery induced displacement of a large number of tribal people and the cash compensation went to the legal non-tribal owners of the land.

Similarly, for the Oil and Natural Gas Corporation (ONGC) township at Nazira, the government acquired 219.65 acres of prime land in Sibsagar district. Besides, the Government of Assam acquired land from time to time as and when needed by public sector companies for oil exploration and construction of oil wells for extraction. For example, ONGC was given 52.94 acres of land in Hailakandi district between 1990–92. And the Government of Assam acquired 81.24 acres of land in North Guwahati to enable a public sector oil company to start a Liquefied Petroleum Gas (LPG) bottling plant.

In constructing the Duliajan–Barauni crude oil pipeline in the late fifties and early sixties of the last century from Upper Assam oilfields to the Barauni Refinery in North Bihar, the government acquired a large amount of land from the people. Official data show that 1,41.34 acres of land have been acquired for the construction of the pipeline in Assam (Fernandes and Bharali 2006: 57). However, the pipeline construction did not induce much displacement because the width of the land acquired was minimal to facilitate the installation of crude oil pipeline.

Now the shadow of the proposed Gas Cracker Project is looming over a large number of people in Lepetkata-Barbaruah area about 12 km away from Dibrugarh township. This project was supposed to start following the Assam Accord 1985 signed between the Government of India and the All Assam Students' Union (AASU). Soon after, the project site was selected at a place called Tengakhat near the oil township of Duliajan in Dibrugarh district with great fanfare with the foundation stone being laid by the Prime Minister of India. It generated tremendous enthusiasm in Assam. But, at a later stage, Tengakhat was abandoned in favour of Lepetkata without specifying any concrete cause. However, it was assumed later that the Ministry of Defence, Government of India, opposed the establishment of such a mega project at a site very near to Chabua Airforce Station on grounds of safety and security. Ultimately, the site was changed to Lepetkata after a long delay.

The famous Reliance Group of Industries was supposed to start this project but recently they backed out from the project after causing a long delay. Now more than 21 years have passed and the project is yet to take off. The government has been trying desperately to find someone from the private sector capable of going in for such a mega project for quite some time. The industrial houses in India are apprehensive of investing in such a mega project because of long-drawn-out insurgency in the state in general and in Dibrugarh and neighbouring Tinsukia district in particular. In the absence of good governance, the industrial houses have to pay a hefty amount to the coffers of various insurgent groups operating in Assam. Even the Tatas had to contribute to the insurgent's coffers. Surinder Paul, brother of the renowned UK-based industrialist of Indian origin Lord Swaraj Paul, had fallen prey to insurgent's bullets. Hence, it became virtually impossible for the government to find some big industrial houses to take up the Gas Cracker Project in Assam. The Reliance Group delayed for too long a period after obtaining the licence without trying to commission the project. Consequently, the project remained in the pipeline for two decades. Ultimately, the Gas Authority of India Limited (GAIL) has been assigned this project. Besides the public sector GAIL, two other public sector enterprises, the Oil India Limited (OIL) and the ONGC are being engaged in this mega project.

The Government of Assam was about to hand over 3,000 *bighas* of land for the project to the Reliance Group. Now the same amount of land is being proposed to be handed over to GAIL. Once the project is implemented, it is going to displace about 50,000 people. Significantly, most of them belong to the Sonowal Kacharis and the *adivasis*. The *adivasis* include the plantation (tea) and ex-plantation labour community. The Sonowal Kacharis are a Scheduled Tribe and the *adivasis* are the 'descheduled' tribe of Assam. Needless to say, these two communities are marginalized communities. It seems the potential displacees are not opposed to their impending displacement provided they are given a reasonably good compensation, resettlement and rehabilitation package. However the matter has not yet been settled and there has been a clear lack of transparency on the part of the state on the subject here as elsewhere in India. Hence, the apprehension of being displaced without proper rehabilitation measures is very strong among the potential displacees. The Tribal Students' Federation and the Assam Tribal Sangha have opposed the acquisition of land by the government and its consequent displacement unless the resettlement and rehabilitation package is placed before the potential displacees. The potential displacees are demanding a transparent, acceptable and humane package from the state.

The threat of involuntary displacement has been hanging on the people of Lepetkata-Barbaruah for a long time. As the project is about to take off the ground, the potential oustees have become increasingly restless. Now they are struggling hard to stop their displacement and demanding the relocation of the project at some other suitable place. They have come out several times to the street *en masse* to protest against the proposed land acquisition and displacement.

This is a new development (*Dainik Agradoot* 2006: 1; Duarah 2006: 1–3). It has been reported that about 50 families living at Lepetkata since 1930 do not have the proper land ownership document, *patta*, hence they are not entitled to any compensation from the government (ibid.). In such cases, the government is proposing cash compensation, not land compensation. Till early August 2006, there was no concrete resettlement and rehabilitation proposal from the state government. In fact, the Government of Assam does not have a clear-cut resettlement and rehabilitation policy for the DPs as well as PAPs.

Consequently, when the government officials went to Lepetkata on 7th September 2006 in order to conduct the land acquisition survey, a large number of potential displacees formed a human barricade and blocked the entry of the officials. In order to break the human barricade, the police opened fire on the gathering and injured 20 protestors (for details, check Our Correspondent 2006: 1 and Our Bureau 2006: 8). Organizations like Sonowal Kachari Yuva Parishad, All Assam Tea-Tribe Students' Association, All Assam Sonowal Kachari Students' Union, Sonowal Kachari Women's Association, Sonowal Kachari National Council and the Krishak Adhikar Dabi Samity and others have reiterated that they are not against the Gas Cracker Project at Lepetkata but want official guarantee so that their legitimate dues are given to them within a fixed time frame (Our Bureau 2006: 8). People have become highly restless and desperate in the absence of a clear-cut resettlement and rehabilitation plan as the district officials are going ahead with their task of land acquisition.

At a time when some of the people of Lepetkata are demanding the shift of the Gas Cracker Project, the MLA from Tinsukia has demanded that the project be commissioned in neighbouring Tinsukia district in view of the opposition of the people of Lepetkata. Besides, some people in Jorhat district are demanding that the project be commissioned at Titabar, the home town of the present Assam Chief Minister (Duarah 2006: 1). However, though the people of Lepetkata-Barbaruah are opposing the location of the project in protest against the absence of a proper resettlement and rehabilitation package for the DPs and the PAPs, the people of Dibrugarh are opposed to the shifting of the project to another district.

The state remained firm on implementing the project. The state government managed to acquire a part of the land needed for the project and handed over the same to GAIL, a few days before the foundation laying ceremony of the project in April 2007 by Dr Manmohan Singh, the Prime Minister of India. Though the construction of the project has formally started, the Assam government is yet to hand over the remaining 462 acres of land to GAIL for the Rs 4,560 crore project (PTI 2007). The state government promised 1,004 acres of land for the project.

Paper Mills

In addition to oil and power sectors, the state became active in establishing paper mills to commercially utilize Assam's forest resources. As a result, the Nagaon Paper Mills (NPM) at Jagiroad situated 56 kilometres from Guwahati, and the Cachar Paper Mills (CPM) at Panchgram came up in the mid-seventies of the last century. Assam already had a big paper mill at Jogighopa in Goalpara district which was established in the late sixties. However, these paper mills have contributed decisively in decreasing the green forest cover, and increasing the level of environmental pollution in Assam. One can very well feel the high level of pollution-induced smell whenever one passes through the paper mill township of Jagiroad.

The NPM, Jagiroad, displaced large number of tribals particularly the Lalung, Tiwa and Karbi tribes. The government acquired 600.84 acres of prime land that mostly belonged to tribals, and was adjacent to the national highway (Bordoloi 1999: 218). The entire land of five villages was acquired for the project and the officials of NPM admitted that the construction of the mill led to the displacement of 84 tribal families to whom they paid compensation (ibid.: 229). These tribal people had to surrender 257.26 acres of their land. The NPM got the required land for establishing the mill from the state. However, the NPM remained silent on the number of non-tribal people displaced from the project area. One can guess the number from the amount of land acquisition from the non-tribal people which stood as high as 343.60 acres (ibid.: 218).

However, the people living around the mills say that the number of DPs is much larger than what has been described by the NPM. Besides, we must note that the tribal people of the project area had large extended families. Those who had fallen within the jurisdiction of the mill had to give in to the state involuntarily. The establishment of NPM increased the pressure on land in and around Jagiroad, which is within 4 to 5 kilometres of the infamous Nellie. One of the root causes of the ghastly Nellie massacre of 1983 was the question of land between a marginalized peasant community of East Bengal origin and a marginalized indigenous tribal community sharing the same living space harmoniously for more than half a century. Development-induced displacement made the tribal people more helpless and frustrated in their traditional homeland. Significantly, this also propelled inter-community conflict in a multi-ethnic society.

A study conducted by the Assam Institute of Research for Tribal and Scheduled Castes found that the compensation paid to the displaced was abysmally low, amounting to Rs 6,300 per *bigha* (0.33 acres) paid in 1982 for homestead and garden land and Rs 2,350 per *bigha* for wet-cultivable land for the village Deosal. However, the compensation paid for another village called Tegheria was Rs 2,500 per *bigha* (0.33 acres) for homestead land and Rs 2,000 per *bigha* for orchards and arable land in 1978 (ibid.: 234). The affected people filed a civil suit in the Gauhati High Court against the value of land acquisitioned from them (ibid.). The people could not fight the case to its logical end because of their economic status. The whole process of land acquisition was very cumbersome for the affected people. The land acquisition started in 1971 and the compensation was paid to the affected people at a much later stage. The affected villagers of Tegheria and Deosal received their compensation amount in 1978 and 1982 respectively.

The study found that the affected people in most cases could not utilize the compensation amount in acquiring assets of permanent nature and further concluded that most of the affected people failed to purchase an alternative plot of land of the same size with the compensation amount, as the value of land in the area had gone up substantially with the progress of commercial activities around the project area (ibid.: 236–237). Obviously, most of the displaced people fell into a cycle of impoverishment. However, 126 persons from the affected people were employed by the NPM as a part of its rehabilitation package. Five villages which had fallen in the project area were ultimately erased fully from history with the beginning of the NPM.

The CPM, Panchgram, also contributed immensely in reducing the bamboo forest cover of the neighbouring North Cachar district and the state of Mizoram. This became a serious threat to the natural forest resources and the community life of the tribal people who inhabit the area. The Tuli Paper Mills established in early eighties at Tuli in the state of Nagaland provides a similar instance. All these paper mills have displaced a large number of people, destabilized their community life, and very significantly affected the rich biodiversity, natural forests and environment of North East India. Moreover, the displaced people did not get adequate compensation, as revealed in the NPM case. A large number of the displaced people were tribal and all of them were pushed to further marginality.

Communication

As the North East is gradually opening up for the rest of India and there is a strong possibility of its opening up with neighbouring countries as a result of India's Look East Policy, a massive displacement of population is likely to take place. Displacement in the absence of a proper resettlement and rehabilitation policy and protection is likely to bring disasters to the ordinary citizens of the North East. This is likely to multiply the number of PAPs in the North East. Obviously most of the victims are going to be tribal. Opening up entails massive construction of new roads and highway networks throughout the North East, besides improving and expanding the existing communication network. While planning for this venture, the decision makers need to look seriously into the question of massive displacement that the communication infrastructure will induce in future. In most cases, infrastructure building induces much more displacement than is generally assumed.

For example, the ongoing construction of the Bogibeel bridge over the river Brahmaputra near Dibrugarh in Upper Assam has caused much larger acquisition of land and consequently much larger displacement. The total length of the bridge is about 4.5 kilometres but the government has acquired more than 2,467 *bighas* of land (roughly more than 800 acres, Hazarika 2005: 25) in order to construct a new rail and a road approach to the bridge. As the project is progressing at a very slow pace and the government is not releasing adequate funds to pay the compensation, a large number of people who have lost their land because of the project are yet to get their compensation. Most of the people who are waiting for their turn for compensation are tribal people of Dhemaji and Dibrugarh districts.

Besides, a large chunk of the national highway is likely to be converted to a four-lane expressway as a part of improving the communication infrastructure and road connectivity in North East India under the Government of India's mega road communication project called 'East-West Corridor'. This ambitious 'Corridor' will connect Silchar in southern Assam with Porabandar in western Gujarat about 3,300 kilometres away with an all-weather four-lane expressway of international standards. The East-West Corridor will stretch over 700 kilometres within the state of Assam alone. The proposed road will be more than four times wider than the existing roads. The project is likely to induce massive displacement of population throughout Assam. The government neither has any resettlement nor a rehabilitation policy for the present and the immediate future generations of the ejected people. Nor does the government have any reasonably scientific estimate of the number of people likely to be displaced in the wake of the expansion of highways in Assam. However, very significantly, the Government of Assam has shown remarkable sensibility in opposing the Government of India's move to build a four-lane expressway in the segment of about 80 kilometres that passes through the Kaziranga National Park in order to protect the animal corridor of the World Heritage Site, well known as the habitat of the endangered one-horned rhino (see Talukdar 2005: 14). But there is no move to provide necessary protection and justice to the potential displaced people.

Additionally, the Asian Highway connecting India and the North East with the South Asian countries and China, is in the pipeline. The Asian Highway is likely to pass through Assam and the North East. This is going to be a mega project in the transport and communication sector in the near future. It seems neither the state nor its marginalized citizens are prepared to face the challenge of its negative consequences. Going by the state's developmental track records and the existing vulnerabilities of the population, this may well turn out to be one of the many developmental misadventures of our time.

Urbanization

Various kinds of developmental activities led to a distorted process of urbanization in the North East. Consequently, it has affected several communities living at the margins of society and economy. Of course, the rate of urbanization in this region is much lower than the all-India average. For example, the percentage of urbanization in Assam is only 12.72 per cent against the all-India average of 27.78 per cent (Census of India 2001). Except the state of Mizoram, the percentage of urbanization in all the remaining six states is far below the all-India average (ibid.). Notwithstanding its slow pace, urbanization has further marginalized the tribal communities.

In 1948, the Government of Assam established the first university of North Eastern India, the Gauhati University, in the outskirt of Guwahati at a place called Jalukbari. In order to establish the university, the Government of Assam acquired a large tract of land from a cluster of Asamiya Muslim villages. This acquisition of land for the sprawling campus of the Gauhati University had displaced a large number of Muslim villagers which reduced them to further marginality. Even today, the villagers allege that they have not received adequate compensation from the government. However, a few persons from the displaced villages got jobs as peons and *chaukidars* in the university.

A similar situation developed when the Government of India started a central university at Silchar in the Barak valley in 1994.

To construct the new university the government acquired 600 acres of land that included 100 acres of private land. This project displaced and severely affected the livelihood of a large number of people from three marginalized communities; Scheduled castes, Karbis and Hmars living in the area. However, on one hand the DPs were provided with small plots of land while on the other the access to CPR was completely blocked with the handover of the acquired land to the new university.

Guwahati, the gateway to the North East, is the largest city in the region. The horizontal urbanization of Guwahati city has displaced the tribal people and forced them to the periphery and margins of city life. The urban expansion of Guwahati has affected two tribal communities—the Karbis and the Bodos—severely. The Karbi tribe that used to inhabit the hills of Chenikuthi-Chandmari-Noonmati-Narangi until sixties and late seventies, have been forced to move out further. Their land has been purchased by the relatively advanced sections of Assamese society. New non-tribal settlements have come up in hitherto tribal areas of Guwahati city. Tribal people have been totally pushed out from these areas. These displaced Karbis now live in the adjoining Bonda-Chandrapur area outside the city boundary in abject poverty. They are, we guess, likely to be pushed out further once the city expands to their present habitat in future. It seems that the urbanization process in Guwahati has been 'community selective' wherein the indigenous tribals have been excluded to the advantage of the non-tribals.

Another very similar case can be cited here. With the carving out of Meghalaya as a new state from the undivided state of Assam, the Government of Assam decided to shift Assam's capital from Shillong to Guwahati in 1973. For this, the government was in need of a large tract of land to establish a new capital and that too very quickly. Here, the choice of the state had fallen on a cluster of tribal villages adjoining Guwahati city. For the state, there was no hurdle in ejecting the tribal people, mostly the Bodos, to construct the new capital. It was relatively easier to displace the tribals than the relatively advanced sections of the non-tribals. Hence, the Bodos had to pay the price for the construction of a new capital. The construction of the new capital complex displaced an estimated 1,00,000 people— nearly all of them tribal. It has been reported that the government acquired about 48,000 acres of land for the new capital. And very significantly more than 43,000 acres of land was a part of the Kamrup tribal belt (Chutia 2005). It has been pointed out that the remaining 5,000 acres of land was used for agricultural purposes wherein the legal *pattadars* used sharecroppers to cultivate the land. Acquisition of this land directly affected the livelihood of the marginalized sharecropper peasants while the cash compensation went to the legal owners of the land (Fernandes and Bharali 2006: 20).

Additionally, the rapid horizontal expansion of Guwahati city affected two other tribal groups, the Karbis and the Rabhas living near the state capital in Kahilipara area. It was a capital lost for the tribal groups. This has happened at a time when the state itself had expressed its concern on the increasing land-alienation among the tribals of North East India in general and the state of Assam in particular.

As the capital was being constructed, the land in and around the new capital 'Dispur' became the prime land in the city. And the relatively advanced sections of Assamese society were successful in buying the land from the tribals in and around the new capital complex. The land market that emerged consequently placed the buyers at an advantage and the sellers at a disadvantage. While what the buyers paid for the land was a relatively low amount for them, what the tribal sellers received was high for them in their perception. Hence, in the process of construction of a new capital, the tribal people were displaced by the state and further dispossessed by the relatively advanced non-tribal sections of the Assamese society. Both ways, the tribal people were displaced from their land simultaneously by the state and the regional dominant class. The tribals were deprived of the benefits of urbanization, proper compensation, proper price and proper rehabilitation. The horizontal expansion of Guwahati city has harmed the tribal immensely.

The process of involuntary displacement is continuing unabated around the city of Guwahati. It has virtually gone unnoticed and undocumented. As per the Assam Accord 1985, the Government of India committed itself to establish its sixth Indian Institute of Technology, popularly known as IIT, in Guwahati. IIT Guwahati became functional in mid-nineties of the last century. In order to construct a new IIT campus at North Guwahati, the state had displaced about 6,000 families and roughly about 35,000 people from their land. Most of the DPs were pushed to the northern side of the IIT campus and a nearby village called Mandakata. As the IITs are fully funded by the Government of India, the state government had to provide the necessary land for the IIT campus. The Government of India released Rs 10.3 crore to the Government of Assam to pay the compensation to the DPs. As per newspaper reports, the Government of Assam released only Rs 4.3 crore to the displaced people till 2001 (*Amar Asam* 2nd September 2001). Here too, the tribal and other economically marginalized people form a large section of the DPs. While the state found it easy to displace these people, the legal absentee landowners usurped the major chunk of the compensation grants while those who found sustenance from them were evicted without it. This brings us to the conclusion that, both the state-sponsored development projects and the process of urbanization have displaced and further marginalized the ordinary masses, particularly the tribal communities in Assam during the post-colonial period.

As Assam was going to host the National Games in the year 2007, a large tract of land had been acquired at a place called Saro-Hojai within the city of Guwahati to build permanent ultra-modern sports stadiums. This, too, induced displacement of several thousand marginalized people in the name of sports which the displaced people neither play nor watch. They have become invisible in the wake of emerging visibility of the imposing stadiums. Now Guwahati can boast of its image for having such massive stadiums with all the facilities that 'modernity' demands while people who were forcibly evicted went into oblivion and were erased from the history of Guwahati forever.

Whatever development has taken place in the North East or for that matter in Guwahati, the gateway to the region, unmistakably reflects the power of the state, not the power of the people. Consequently, a large number of people have been evicted from their land and ejected from their shelter and livelihood. Here, the development process itself has become an instrument of aggression for a large number of marginalized people.

3

Hard-hitting Reality

Development-induced Displacement of
Population in Post-colonial Assam

The state is the most powerful political institution in a democracy.
In addition to its 'legitimate' right to use violence, it has also reserved
a crucial right for itself; the monopoly to acquire land in the 'overriding public interest'. This has virtually evolved as a monopoly right
in the field. Both the colonial and post-colonial Indian state used this
right with impunity, virtually without any question raised for a long
time. However, land is increasingly becoming a scarce commodity
today, and for many it is the only source of survival. Snatching away
land forcibly from such people degrades their lives and livelihood
and makes them rootless and destitute. It directly attacks their dignity
and further heightens their marginality. Now, because of gradual
sharpening of democratic consciousness, many people have started
questioning the state's right to acquire the land of its citizens as a matter
of one-sided right. The meaning of overriding public interest is always
a matter of opinion and subject to contestation, where one interpret-
ation may be diametrically opposite to the other. If the state decides
something in the 'overriding public interest', and the people do not
accept it as such, then it becomes a serious problem of conflict between the state and the people. The state cannot ignore the views of
its own people and therefore it is important to build a new mechan-
ism to resolve such conflict within a democratic and humane framework. If the state acquires land, and displaces people in the public
interest, it immediately becomes a moral responsibility for the state
in any democratic society to resettle and rehabilitate the displaced

people at a level definitely not lower than their pre-displacement status. The state cannot abrogate its moral and ethical responsibilities towards its citizens. But it very often abrogates its responsibilities. The same thing has happened to the people displaced by various development projects during the post-colonial period in India. Assam or North East is no exception to this trend started by the colonial regime and pursued vigorously by the post-colonial state as an essential part of its modernity and nation-building project.

Land Acquisition and Displacement

The state acquires private land through its own legal process. In India, most land acquisition by the states has taken place under the provisions of the colonial law called Land Acquisition Act (LAQ) 1894. This Act has been backing up the state as its legal resource against common people. It provides all the necessary immunities to the state against its people. This law not only enables the state to acquire privately owned land for so called public purposes, but also to displace/evict people from their land, home and livelihood very arbitrarily. The legal provisions of the LAQ 1894 very clearly reveal the class-character of not only the colonial state, but of the post-colonial state also.

Though the state goes in for land acquisition in the 'public interest', the LAQ 1894 has not clearly defined it. 'Public interest' remains vague and confusing. Under the provisions of the LAQ 1894, the government can issue a notification for land acquisition, and allow the affected people to file complaints/objections within two months of first notification. The second notification deals with the complaints/objections and gives a final decision. The third step is the award that decides the compensation and other related issues about the land to be acquired. For the first two stages, the government is required to issue the gazette notifications (see Ramanathan 1999). Besides, the LAQ 1894 has certain urgency and emergency provisions that empower the government to take over private land within just 15 days under the urgency provision and within 48 hours under the emergency provisions. This law deals with private land and significantly there is no clear-cut law for the acquisition of land that comes under the CPRs. Land under the CPR is regarded as the property of the state. Hence, the case of acquisition of land under CPRs is done through the Government Order (GO) or Inter-departmental Agreement. Fernandes and Bharali (2006: 4) have observed that while LAQ empowers the state to acquire the private land it does not recognize the CPRs as people's sustenance. The government pays some compensation to the private owners whose land has been acquired but when the land is acquired from the CPRs, the affected people are not entitled to any compensation except-ing the areas that come under the Sixth Schedule of the Indian Constitution. Needless to say, those who are entitled to compensa-tion do not receive compensation in time due to the cumbersome procedure. Obviously, there is no provision for resettlement and rehabilitation of the displaced people who have lost their home, land and livelihood in the public interest. It needs to be recollected here that a major chunk of the DPs and PAPs in India are tribal people. Prabhu (1998: 247) has observed

> The Colonial Land Acquisition Act 1894, freely permits the state to alienate tribal land for public purpose. It is not simply that the state enjoys a superior right but it can conveniently convert it into an absolute right while alienating tribal lands.

Now the question comes whether an antiquarian land acquisition law enforced in a colony by the colonial regime in the interest of the colonizer more than a century and a decade ago, can still be enforced in a post-colonial structure of freedom and democracy wherein the relationship between the state and its colonial subjects has transformed into a relationship between the state and its citizens. Ideally, all colonial subjects should have become citizens in the post-colonial situation. However, in reality this has not happened. There exists a significant deficit in the popular participation of citizens in Indian democracy. A large number of citizens are still located at the colonial stage of being the subjects of the state, not participant citizens. This law is still being enforced to evict people and snatch their land in the 'overriding public interest'.

In addition to the eviction, Petterson observed:

> ... victims of development-induced displacement often have their rights violated afterwards. Many are left landless and destitute. If the displaced are not properly resettled and rehabilitated, it is irrelevant whether the project forcing them off their land is an 'overriding public interest' or not. The rights have still been violated. In 1994, the Indian government reported that 10 million displaced were still 'awaiting rehabilitation'. Most researchers would argue that this figure is far too low. Some would suggest that a very few of the 21–33 million development-induced IDPs in India have had their livelihood restored (2002A: 115).

Modernity has been at the core of the mainstream discourse on development in post-colonial India. The whole process of modernization has been very painful for the Indian masses. There were successful attempts at demonstrating the conspicuous mega projects like big dams as the symbol of development, power and modernity in India. In most cases, development projects in India take into consideration only the technical and financial aspects of a project; they virtually ignore the social, political, cultural, and human aspects of it. Hence, most development projects become very brutal against marginalized people and instead of rescuing people from marginalization, they push the people further into marginality. And consequently, the human/ethical question of justice gets ignored totally. This led to the passing of a milestone judgement by the Supreme Court of India as early as in 1982. It observed very explicitly:

> Before any development project is taken up, the social cost involved must be evaluated with a view to balancing the advantages.... Every development programme must provide for simultaneous rehabilitation of the persons who are thrown out of their land and houses on account of acquisition of land for such developmental projects. No developmental project, however laudable, can possibly justify impoverishment of large sections of people and their utter destitution (Supreme Court of India 1982).

Similarly, the National Human Rights Commission (henceforth NHRC) in its annual report 2000–01 had spelt out its view that there was a need to formulate a revised national policy to deal with greater sensitivity, the issues concerning the rehabilitation of people affected by mega projects. Specifically, the Commission expressed the opinion that the resettlement and rehabilitation of persons displaced through the acquisition of land for various projects should form part of the provision of the LAQ itself, or be the subject of appropriate separate legislation, so that they are bound within legal parameters. The commission was additionally of the view that the government should, while adopting a comprehensive policy, provide for that policy to itself be incorporated into appropriate legislation within a specific time frame (National Human Rights Commission 2002: 88). The NHRC further observes:

> The Commission takes this opportunity to urge, again, that the National Policy to be adopted in this respect must be based on principles that are fair, just and transparent and that conform with the Constitution and the treaty obligations of this country, particularly ILO convention 107, to which India is a party and which provides for the protection of the rights of the indigenous and tribal people (ibid.: 89).

Despite such observations from the NHRC, we do not see any significant qualitative change in the attitude of the state towards the displaced people anywhere in India. However, the NHRC observation supports the demands of anti-dam movements for proper and dignified resettlement and rehabilitation of the IDPs. It has given recognition to the problem of development-induced displacement as a right issue in India. This is a very significant development in the 'rights discourse' in India.

It needs to be pointed out explicitly that a Right-based Approach (henceforth RBA) to development includes the following fundamental elements (Marks: 2004: 25 quoted from website of UNHCHR):

* express linkage to rights
* accountability
* empowerment
* participation
* non-discrimination and attention to vulnerable groups.

Firstly, in the RBA, the aims and objectives of development need to be defined explicitly in terms of particular right as legally enforceable entitlements for the citizens. The RBA is a convergence between human rights and development so as to protect the people from developmental aggression and injustice. Secondly, accountability is fundamental to the RBA. The state as a 'duty holder' must protect the rights of the 'right holders', that is the citizens. It implies that the RBA can operate only within definite institutional provisions in terms of adequate laws and policies, administrative structure and mechanisms of redressal. Thirdly, RBA aims at providing the citizens with the power, capacity, capability and access needed to change their lives, improve their own communities and influence their destinies. Next, it stresses on the participation of civil society groups, informal groups and individuals, minorities, indigenous people, women and all other stakeholders in the development process. And lastly, RBA gives special attention to the weaker and the vulnerable sections of the society so as to improve their status through the process of development. It emphasizes that all the developmental activities must be non-discriminatory in nature (see OHCHR 2001). Simply speaking, development must ensure protection and promotion of citizens' rights; it must empower the citizens besides ensuring the participation of the citizens in the planning, implementing and monitoring of development projects; and the state must be accountable for its developmental activities.

Unfortunately, RBA is yet to become a part of development discourse in India. Consequently, the rights of the common people are not there in the development agenda. Hence, in many cases the process of development itself violates the rights of people instead of enhancing their rights and capabilities. The mainstream development discourse lacks accountability on the part of the state; in most cases, it neither empowers nor ensures the participation of the people. It is a top-down centralized process. Besides, it is highly regimented in nature. In many cases, it discriminates against the vulnerable groups. On the other hand, the state has not shown any sensitivity to people living at the periphery of the country and at the margins of society. For both tribal and non-tribal people in North East India, land is the most crucial resource. And the state can take over land from any person whenever it feels it is in the 'overriding public interest'. For development one needs space—land. Under the existing discourse, even if the land is already occupied, it is to be vacated and people are to be ejected, if necessary, by brute force, from their land, home and livelihood in order to make way for development! In such a framework, development becomes more important for the state than the people. It excludes people who suffer for such projects. This propels a series of encounters, sometimes in manifest form and sometimes in latent form, between the state and its own citizens on the question of development. Development becomes a site of contestation. It tests the power of the state and the people. This contestation activates the emerging politics of development.

Notwithstanding this, the possible conflict between the state and people is avoidable provided the right-framework for all the state-sponsored development projects is adopted at the beginning on one hand, and includes a sustainable resettlement and rehabilitation measures as a part of the development project on the other. This will enhance the credibility of the state and erase the conflict on development issues between the state and the people. In the process, development will have a humane face which has been sadly missing in the existing development paradigm.

Quantification of Displacement

In this part of the study, we propose to look into the quantitative aspects of development-induced displacement in the North Eastern state of Assam. But how do we look at it? It is an arduous task in the absence of a reliable database on the Indian as well as the Assam situation. To understand the Assam situation is much more difficult in the virtual absence of proper data. The government does not maintain a proper database on displacement or on resettlement and rehabilitation. The press does not look upon it as a serious problem. The social science community has not given it the kind of attention it deserves. Hence, we do not have adequate and authentic data to depend on in order to analyze the empirical situation with a high degree of precision. Consequently, in the absence of empirical data and records, we have attempted to collect and generate some data in order to understand the quantitative aspect of the problem.

Here, we have attempted to collect data on land acquisition by the Government of Assam through the gazette notifications for different developmental activities and for which the government paid some compensation to legal landowners. Besides, we have looked for information from the offices of the Deputy Commissioners of all the districts of Assam. We need to state here emphatically that there exists severe incongruity between these two sets of official data. Data collected from the offices of the Deputy Commissioners shows a larger quantum of land acquisition than what has been revealed by the data in the Government Gazette notifications. Through this route, we have tried to collect data on the empirical situation of land acquisition and its consequent population displacement in Assam. Of course, such data does not include all the government land that was allotted for various kinds of development activities. However, we must point out that our data is not absolutely complete and obviously inadequate to quantify the entire situation exactly. Notwithstanding such problems, the data we are presenting here on the land acquisition reflects unmistakably the enormity of the problem.

However, it is more difficult to gather the displacement data from government sources. In most cases the government officials and political class do not accept the very concept of 'Displacement'. Dwivedi (2002: 709–32) pointed out very pertinently that:

> Displacement is a harsher term which politicians and administrators want to avoid as it encapsulates the act of displacement.... Resettlement on the other hand emphasizes some positive actions towards damage control by setting up various programmes to rehabilitate those who were affected by development activity.

Most government officials can/do not distinguish between resettlement and rehabilitation. Instead they use words like relief and compensation. They are allergic to concepts like displacement, which have been widely used throughout the globe including UN agencies and social science communities. In such a situation, one can imagine the difficult task of collecting the data on displacement of population. Hence, we find it is very difficult to gather data on the displacement of population in India. Consequently, though this is not the best method, one has to depend on extrapolation of data from different sources in order to quantify the problem. Simply speaking, gathering the land acquisition data is difficult, and more difficult is to gather data on its consequence, that is, displacement of population.

We need to admit here that all land acquisitions might not have generated cent per cent displacement of population. On the other hand, many people who were actually displaced by land acquisition have not been reflected in the data because we have been able to include only those who received some compensation from the government. A large number of displaced persons were not entitled to any compensation as per existing laws because they were technically not the legal owner of the land/*pattadar* despite being the occupants for a long time! Nevertheless, the data we are presenting here would enable us to situate and understand, in a however limited way, the enormity of the problem of development-induced displacement of population in an underdeveloped state like Assam.

DPs and PAPs

Before we embark upon the quantification exercise here, it would be necessary to explain briefly the concept of DPs and PAPs. When we talk of DPs, we refer to those people who have lost their homes/shelter, land and livelihood consequent upon acquisition of land by the state for its own use or on behalf of others whom the state wants to grant the land. In other words, the DPs are forced to leave their home/shelter and relocate themselves elsewhere. Of course, all the DPs may not be able to relocate themselves. They may not find any resettlement and rehabilitation opportunities at all. Instead, they may become poorer. Here lies their risks, vulnerability and threat to their basic human rights as citizens. Micheal M. Cernea (2000: 3659–78) rightly locates a set of eight interrelated impoverishment risks/vulnerabilities of the DPs as landlessness, joblessness, homelessness, marginalization, food insecurity, increased morbidity, loss of access to

CPRs and social disarticulation. Post-displacement, most of the DPs experienced these unavoidable vulnerabilities. Obviously, these DPs are IDPs in terms of definitions of the United Nations Guiding Principles on Internal Displacement (UN 1999) and other international humanitarian laws and relevant instruments.

> ... development induced displacement in India shows the unsustainability of attempts to draw distinction between IDPs and DIDs (development-induced displacees). DIDs in India undergo violation of human rights at the hands of their national and state governments and deserve to be treated as IDPs ... (Velath 2003: 37).

The major distinction between the DPs and PAPs, however, lies in the question of physical relocation. Unlike DPs, the PAPs do not experience the problem of physical relocation and stay wherever they have been living prior to the land acquisition for the new development project. However, such projects may affect some people who may lose some of their land and means of sustenance. For example, if some people are dependent on a CPR for their sustenance and their access to it is blocked as a consequence of land acquisition for development projects then they are bound to suffer deeply. Such projects directly affect their lives and livelihood very significantly without affecting their shelter. In India, various development projects have been generating both DPs and PAPs. Depending on the nature of the development project, it may generate either or both categories simultaneously as a consequence of land acquisition and its subsequent occupation by a new owner. In the absence of proper resettlement, the DPs suffer most, while in the absence of proper rehabilitation both DPs and PAPs suffer simultaneously.

Resettlement and Rehabilitation

Before moving further, it would be necessary to briefly touch upon the concept of resettlement and rehabilitation, which are intrinsically related to the question of land acquisition and its consequent displacement of population. Development is a spatial activity that modifies as well as redistributes space. In the process many people get displaced from their land, shelter and livelihood. Robbed of these three by state or any non-state factor, these people become landless, shelterless, jobless and significantly, identityless. We have also pointed out earlier Micheal Cernea's impoverishment risks for the DPs and the PAPs. If proper resettlement and rehabilitation measures are not adopted, the DPs and the PAPs are certain to experience greater impoverishment in the post-land acquisition period.

Displaced people require resettlement. Here, resettlement means one-off physical relocation of the DPs at some other place after they are forced out of the project area. Two fundamental conditions for resettlement are to provide adequate land and shelter for the DPs. Rehabilitation means giving social, cultural, community and economic support/livelihood protection for the DPs and PAPs in the aftermath of displacement. There would not have been so much of hue and cry had there been a practice of providing a sustainable resettlement and rehabilitation package to the DPs and PAPs in India. It is the lack of proper rehabilitation and resettlement support that has brought to the fore the question of development-induced displacement as an issue of right and justice.

Oliver-Smith observed very cogently in this regard:

One of the voices increasingly heard today is that of people displaced and resettled by development projects. Uprooting and displacement have been among the central experiences of modernity (Oliver-Smith 2001: 4).

He further observed that the resettlement process itself

is one of the most acute expressions of powerlessness because it constitutes a loss of control over one's physical space. The only thing left is the loss of body (ibid.).

It needs to be noted that the poor, indigenous people and other marginalized groups in the face of efforts to displace them are,

…increasingly choosing to resist displacement in the hope that it will prove more effective in protecting their long-term interest than cooperation (Fisher 1999).

Now it is possible to understand the nature of the state by understanding its role in the development process. Development tells, very pertinently, the class-character of the state. This has also provided a critique of India's post-colonial development paradigm. Displacement is the first and the most decisive issue that propelled popular resistance, or call it a people's movement, throughout India. North East India, too, is no exception to this trend. Later on, other issues like sustainability, ecological degradation and the rights were added which energized the people's movement very significantly. Now we can see slow and gradual emergence of such movements in North East too against many state-sponsored mega development projects. We propose to look into such movements in chapter four; here in this chapter we are looking into the quantum of land acquisition in Assam and its consequent generation of DPs and PAPs during the post-colonial period.

A. Land Acquisition at the Dawn of Independence

The Refugee Flow

Refugee issue is not a development issue *per se*, yet we have taken it up for a brief scrutiny mainly because it led to massive land acquisition and generated DPs and PAPs consequently. Following independence and the partition in 1947, both India and Pakistan experienced massive flow of refugees, one of the largest flows of population in the world history. Creation of East Pakistan had severe effects in Eastern India including Assam. There was a massive inflow of East Pakistani refugees to West Bengal, Tripura and Assam. Similarly, there was an outflow of Indian refugees to Pakistan. In the aftermath of partition, a large number of Bengali Hindus migrated from East Pakistan to West Bengal and many Bengali Muslims migrated from West Bengal to East Pakistan. Similarly, a large number of Bengali Muslims of the Barak valley were forced to migrate to East Pakistan and a large number of Bengali Hindus were forced to leave East Pakistan.

Soon after independence and the partition in 1947, not only the state border but even the border of a sub-division/district became an international boundary. Provincial boundaries between East Bengal and undivided Assam's Lushai Hill District, United Khasi and Jaintia Hill District and the undivided Goalpara District, all of a sudden, transformed into a long international boundary. Independence also led to partition of undivided Assam's Sylhet district, with a large chunk of it going to East Pakistan through a referendum. Partition severely affected the people of the Barak valley wherein the Hindu–Muslim division had been sharp, where a boundary of a sub-division transformed into an international boundary. In a situation of suspicion, violence, threat of violence and fear, large number of people from East Pakistan came to Assam particularly from Sylhet to Cachar district and vice versa.

It is very difficult to ascertain the actual number of refugees in Assam. According to a report, the percentage of people of foreign origin in Assam including Sylhet was 5.6 per cent of its total population (Srivastava 1979: XIV). Luthra (1972) points out that 52.83 lakh of refugees came to India from East Pakistan out of which West Bengal accommodated 39.56 lakh. The remaining 13 lakh were accepted by other states. Misra (1985: 13) has estimated that Assam had received 6.87 lakh of East Pakistani refugees. A large number of them came to Cachar and Dhubri districts adjoining East Pakistan.

It needs to be kept in mind that the refugee flow from East Pakistan which started at the time of independence continued, of course at different rates, from time to time till East Pakistan was erased from history in 1971. According to Rao, Assam received 3.90 lakh of displaced persons from East Pakistan till 1956 (Rao 1974). And according to Nag, by 1961 about 2.10 lakh and by 1968 another 4.5 lakh are reported to have entered and settled down in Assam permanently (Nag 2006: 129). However, in the wake of the liberation struggle of Bangladesh an unprecedented 1 crore refugees entered India and some of them did not go back to Bangladesh after its liberation and settled down permanently in West Bengal, Assam and Tripura. By extrapolating the earlier refugees and their natural growth rate, Nag estimated the refugee population in North East India at about 15 lakh in total (ibid.).

Table 3.1 depicts a partial portion of land used for the refugee resettlement projects in Assam's plains. For seven such projects, the
government of Assam acquired 5,602.46 acres of land. Among all
these projects, the Sonitpur project acquired the highest amount of
land for rehabilitation of refugees. However, the gazettes record
acquisition of 16,297.9 acres of land in Cachar district alone to resettle
3,150 refugee families, which means an average of 5.17 acres of land
for each refugee family (Fernandes and Bharali 2006: 72).

TABLE 3.1
Land Used for Some Refugee Rehabilitation Projects 1947–2000

Projects	Districts	Decade	Land	Sources
Refugee Rehab	Cachar	1947–60	742.24	Deputy Commissioner Cachar 1948A, 1948B, 1953A.
Krishnagar Camp	Dhubri	1951–60	4.44	Deputy Commissioner Dhubri 1958C
Refugee Rehab	Barpeta	1961–70	93.53	Assam Gazettes 1947–50
Refugee Camp	Darrang	1947–60	613.92	Assam Gazettes 1947–50
E & D Refugees	Dibrugarh	1951–70	115.01	Assam Gazettes 1947–50
Refugee Rehab	Kamrup	1947–60	751.75	Assam Gazettes 1947–50
Refugee Rehab	Sonitpur	1947–70	3,281.57	Assam Gazettes 1947–50
Total	**7 districts**		**5,602.46**	

Assam not only received refugees from East Pakistan, it also received refugees from Tibet in the wake of the Dalai Lama's escape
from Tibet. It has been reported that 1,800 Tibetan refugee families
were resettled at Missamari in Sonitpur district and 3,000 families
of partition refugees were resettled at Tamulpur in Kamrup district
(Subba 2003: 132). Besides, 10,000 Garo families were also resettled
in the Karbi-Anglong Hill district (Sagar 2005: 1). The Government
of Assam resettled 3,150 refugee families from East Pakistan in the
Cachar district (Fernandes and Bharali 2006: 72). All this put together, the Government of Assam resettled 17,950 refugee families
in Assam (ibid.: 72). However, on the basis of extrapolation, Fernandes
and Bharali estimated the number of refugee families that entered
Assam at 70,000 (ibid.: 72). As we have seen earlier in this section,
on an average, a refugee family was allotted 5.17 acres of land as a
resettlement package. From this clue, Fernandes and Bharali estimated that the Government of Assam acquired 3,50,000 acres of land
for refugee resettlement in Assam, calculating at an average 5 acres

for each refugee family (ibid.: 72). According to them, the government acquired 16,297.26 acres of private land, and 3,33,703 acres of land from CPRs. This kind of massive land acquisition obviously generated a large number of DPs and PAPs in Assam. However, the government records do not reflect this in any significant manner. It has been estimated from the extrapolated data that land acquisition for refugee resettlement in Assam generated 1,46,500 DPs and 1,37,000 PAPs, totalling to a massive 2,83,500 persons in the host society (ibid.: 102). Here, the most significant contradiction is that the state, in order to resettle a group of displaced persons, displaces another group of persons belonging to the host community(ies). This is perhaps unprecedented in the history of resettlement wherein to resettle a group of DPs another group of DPs is simultaneously generated.

B. Land Acquisition: Defence and Security Purpose

In the earlier part of this study, there is a brief mention about the geo-strategic situation in which Assam has been located. The partition of India severely affected the communication network of entire North East with the rest of India. The frontier status of the North East was further deepened by the creation of East Pakistan. Consequently, a large tract of provincial and even district boundaries transformed into international boundaries all of a sudden. This substantially elongated the international border of the North East. The post-colonial compulsions to meet the defence and security requirements under a qualitatively changed geo-strategic situation, led the state to acquire a large tract of land from the people of Assam. The people had no alternative but to part with their land at a compensation decided and given by the state.

However, we need to recollect that geo-strategically North East emerged as an important region for the British Indian State. In the wake of the Second World War, the colonial government had to build several bases for the army besides constructing several airports in Assam. A large contingent of the British Indian army and the army of the Allied Forces were stationed in Assam in the face of the threat from the Japanese army and the *Azad Hind Fauj*. Very significantly, at one stage the Japanese army advanced near Kohima, the present day capital of Nagaland, and certain areas of Manipur. The preparation for war led to massive land acquisition in Assam at the fag end of the colonial period. Hence, we see that because of geo-strategic compulsions, the colonial government acquired a large tract of land for its armed forces prior to India's independence. These lands and establishments were transferred to the Ministry of Defence, Government of India, at the time of transfer of power in 1947 following independence. However, land acquisition did not stop at that stage though there had been a halt in the initial years after independence (1947–50). Instead, thereafter, land acquisition in Assam increased for the defence establishments in the wake of changed geo-strategic equations.

Table 3.2 demonstrates the quantum of land acquired by the state from Assam's 23 districts for various defence establishments. From the data, one can imagine the quantum of total land acquisition in the entire state and region. One can observe the quantum jump in land acquisition from 790.63 acres in the decade 1951–60 to a massive 5,135.69 acres in the decade 1961–70. Land acquisition has been highest in Kamrup urban district and second highest in the Sonitpur district. This was a crucial period for the people of North East, because India fought two battles from this frontier region; one against China in 1962 and the other against Pakistan in 1971 in the wake of the liberation struggle of Bangladesh. Guwahati, the headquarters of the Kamrup urban district, is the gateway to North East India; hence there were significant land acquisitions in Guwahati for defence and security purposes. On the other hand, Sonitpur district is located at a strategically important junction. This district is adjacent to Kameng district of Arunachal Pradesh, part of the erstwhile NEFA. The Chinese army virtually occupied the entire Kameng district and reached the foothills adjoining Sonitpur district in 1962. For the NEFA front, the Government of India established several military establishments in Sonitpur district. Table 3.2 also demonstrates that the land acquisition in Barpeta district was lowest, followed by Hailakandi and Golaghat districts. These three districts did not have strategic importance for the state. Preparation for the two wars led to very significant land acquisition in Assam; and consequently displacement of

TABLE 3.2
Decade-wise Land Acquisition for Defence Establishments 1947–2000 (in acres) in Assam

District	1947–50	1951–60	1961–70	1971–80	1981–90	1991–2000	NA	Total
Dhubri	0	4.76	16.12	2.12	0	91.27	10.85	125.12
Kokrajhar	4.24	2.3	271.38	117.09	40.23	8.75	0	439.75
Bangaigaon	0	0	32.67	32.67	0	0	0	69.58
Goalpara	0	3.2	0	10.16	0	0.79	0	14.15
Barpeta	0	0	0	3.33	2.67	0	0	6
Nalbari	0.67	0	2.3	2.48	12.95	1.45	0	19.85
Kamrup	0	501.69	3,519.42	479.81	200.66	51.81	34.03	4,787.42
Darrang	0	0	0	27.79	4.42	0	0	32.21
Sonitpur	0	205.71	676.65	460.81	17.38	29.77	0	1,390.32
Lakhimpur	0	0	0.51	90.04	0	0	0	90.55
Dhemaji	0	0	0	0	0.91	0	0	0.91
Morigaon	0	0	0	0	0	0	0	0
Nagaon	0	0.27	0	79.42	0	1.42	0	81.11
Golaghat	0	0.52	3.33	0.33	0	3.62	0	7.8
Jorhat	0	43.98	7.53	200.75	0.23	0.42	0	252.91
Sibsagar	1.45	0	361.3	0	0	0	0	362.75
Dibrugarh	0.33	0.91	92.04	252.7	49.98	0	0	395.96
Tinsukia	0	0	87.21	21.59	0	0	0	108.8
Karbi Anglong	0	0	3.02	4.3	3.23	0	2.04	12.59
N.C. Hills	0	0	0	0	0	0	0	0
Karimganj	0	13.65	38.59	30.37	10.72	14.76	39.16	147.25
Hailakandi	0	0	0	0	0	0	6.66	6.66
Cachar	0	13.64	23.62	193.61	335.18	85	88.62	739.67
Assam	**6.69**	**790.63**	**5,135.69**	**2,009.37**	**678.56**	**289.06**	**181.36**	**9,091.36**

Source: Government of Assam, Assam Gazettes 1947–2000.

population. Quite a few defence establishments located in Assam's plains can boast of having luxurious golf courses meant for their officers. One can, however, distinctly see that once the threat of military conflict ceased, there has been a very drastic reduction of the land acquisition rate in the subsequent decades.

Additionally, the state has been involved in two little internal wars, one against the Naga and the other against the Mizo insurgents. In order to combat insurgency in the Naga and Mizo Hills, the army engaged in regrouping the tribal villages in the insurgency-affected regions. This forcibly displaced a large number of tribals from their ancestral villages. This severely affected the community life and livelihood of the tribals. At a later stage, though the Mizo insurgency ceased to exist, yet innumerable insurgencies emerged in the entire North East. Following the path of Naga and Mizo insurgencies, strong insurgent groups emerged in Manipur, Assam and Tripura from the early eighties of the 19th century. Insurgent groups emerged even among the smaller ethnic groups throughout the North East. All this contributed towards further militarization of the region. After Jammu and Kashmir, the North East is obviously the most militarized region in India. Needless to say, displacement of local population is obviously a part and parcel of any militarization process and the North East is no exception to this trend.

It needs to be pointed out that though we have shown the amount of land acquisition for defence establishments in Assam during the period 1947–2000 at 9,091.36 acres in Table 3.2, there are reasons to believe that the actual acquisition/occupation is much larger. What we have shown here is from the gazette notifications only. It is very difficult to get an accurate picture about the land acquisition for defence establishments because these projects are treated as secrets for 'national security' reasons. A recent study has estimated that 26,404.51 acres of land has been in use for defence and security purpose in Assam (Fernandes and Bharali 2006: 62).

In addition to defence from external threats, the state had also gone in for land acquisition for internal security purposes. The presence of various security forces is quite visible in the North East compared to the rest of India, of course with the exception of Jammu and Kashmir. Once the threat of war from external sources ceased in this region, threat to the Indian state started from internal sources. North East India remained a politically sensitive and disturbed region for a long time. In the face of bad governance and deterioration of law and order situation virtually in all the North Eastern states, the concentration of paramilitary forces and expansion of other police forces took place. All this led to further land acquisition in Assam during the later part of the 20th century when the land acquisition rate substantially decreased for the defence forces.

Table 3.3 depicts the quantum of displacement by representative defence and security projects in seven select districts of Assam, not for the whole state. It shows that these projects displaced 1,035 persons and affected 11,789 persons. As the total data for the entire state is not available, it would not be wrong to assume safely that the actual number of DPs and PAPs is much larger for Assam. In a recently completed research project, Walter Fernandes and Gita Bharali (2006: 90–91) estimated the number of DPs and PAPs caused by the defence and security establishments in Assam at 3,337 and 37,083 respectively or a total of 40,420 persons.

C. Environment Protection

The Government of Assam acquired a large tract of land under the environment protection category of developmental activities during the period 1947 to 2000. This category includes Assam's famous national parks and wildlife sanctuaries on one hand; and soil conservation, embankment and drainage systems on the other. Besides it also includes components such as zoos, museums and other areas meant to protect natural as well as human made heritage. Table 3.4 demonstrates that altogether 46,004.2 acres of land was acquired from the people as per the gazette notifications of the Government of Assam during the period 1947–2000. Needless to say, Assam is a flood-prone state; hence high emphasis was given to the projects that aimed at controlling flood. Excepting two hill districts, all the districts in Assam's plains have been vulnerable to recurring floods and river bank erosion.

A major chunk of this land was acquired for the purpose of controlling flood in Assam's plain areas. Hence, we can see that the land acquisition under this category is lowest in North Cachar Hill

TABLE 3.3
DPs/PAPs of Some Representative Defence and Security Projects

Project	District	DPs	PAPs	Total	Sources/File details
Cachar Watch Post	Cachar	0	704	704	Deputy Commissioner, Cachar 1972E
BSF Head Quarters	Cachar	0	61	61	Deputy Commissioner, Cachar 1976C, 1996A
Rongpur Police Outpost	Cachar	220	22	242	Deputy Commissioner, Cachar 1971C
Dwarbang Police Outpost	Cachar	0	1,161	1,161	Deputy Commissioner, Cachar 1966A
Tarapur Town Outpost	Cachar	231	688	919	Deputy Commissioner, Cachar 1953B
District Jail	Hailakandi	0	50	50	Deputy Commissioner, Hailakandi 1990B
Border Security Force	Kamrup urban	0	336	336	Deputy Commissioner, Kamrup (Urban) 1983G
Defence for Army	Kamrup urban	28	4,169	4,197	Deputy Commissioner, Kamrup (Urban) 1963C, 1975A, 1981C
Battalion Head Quarters	Kamrup urban	0	193	193	Deputy Commissioner, Kamrup (Urban) 1972D, 1983A, 1984A
Airforce Barzar	Kamrup urban	220	1,716	1,936	Deputy Commissioner, Kamrup (Urban) 1999B
87 BSF Head Quarters	Karimganj	0	110	110	Deputy Commissioner, Karimganj 1971D, 1983D
District Jail Nalbari	Nalbari	0	215	215	Deputy Commissioner, Nalbari 1978D
Tezpur Airforce	Sonitpur	0	633	633	Deputy Commissioner, Sonitpur 1964C, 1970A, 1970E, 1989A
Defence Purpose Army	Sonitpur	336	1,093	1,429	Deputy Commissioner, Sonitpur 1960D, 1969C, 1979B
Project Vortek	Sonitpur	0	121	121	Deputy Commissioner, Sonitpur 1961C, 1961D, 1961E, 1962A, 1988I
Project Tusker	Sonitpur	0	88	88	Deputy Commissioner, Sonitpur. 1961B
Field Firing Range	Sonitpur	0	198	198	Deputy Commissioner, Sonitpur 1968A
Transit Camp	Kamrup Rural	0	231	231	Deputy Commissioner. Kamrup (Rural) 1965A
Total		**1,035**	**11,789**	**12,824**	

Source: Government of Assam.

TABLE 3.4

Decade-wise Land Acquisition for Environment Protection 1947–2000

District	1947–50	1951–60	1961–70	1971–80	1981–90	1991–2000	NA	Total
Dhubri	0	142.56	237.06	648.79	194.25	286.34	345.46	1,854.46
Kokrajhar	0	0	271.38	117.09	53.44	68.77	0	510.68
Bongaigaon	0	5.76	228.59	84.29	8.13	0	29.54	356.31
Goalpara	0	59.14	1,313.39	85.17	103.28	383.87	133.75	2,078.6
Barpeta	11.17	84.17	1,202.44	1,416.06	984.97	488.88	0	4,187.69
Nalbari	0	466.72	975.77	1,096.42	237.85	117.22	64.9	2,958.88
Kamrup	63.43	637.81	1,307.57	1,020.5	1,123.53	185.37	349.16	4,687.37
Darrang	0	74.05	660.57	1,008.06	248.5	127.02	1.78	2,119.98
Sonitpur	0	584.2	718.47	1,214.44	126.53	201.1	24.35	2,869.09
Lakhimpur	0	39.08	1,443.7	1,398.01	143.65	126.27	10.7	3,161.41
Dhemaji	121.15	121.15	277.3	303.18	137.31	255.62	20.48	1,236.19
Morigaon	21.14	492.77	323.8	345.37	258.12	0	0	1,441.2
Nagaon	0.83	251.49	2,538.93	762.89	58.96	470.82	0	4,083.92
Golaghat	0	264.41	690.58	298.4	261.11	3.77	82.66	1,600.93
Jorhat	0	206.47	583.49	291.28	2.75	14.72	0	1,098.71
Sibsagar	14.09	648.47	445.27	631.85	243.67	13.3	160.31	2,156.96
Dibrugarh	0	749.58	681.43	420.03	173.96	60.86	0	2,085.86
Tinsukia	0	209.52	53.88	0	0	0	0	263.4
K Anglong	0	0	3.72	417.06	212.07	58.4	169.98	861.23
N.C. Hills	0	0	0	0	58.56	64.22	0	122.78
Karimganj	2.67	101.84	185.46	575.11	186.25	10.56	0	1,061.89
Hailakandi	0	8.3	283.62	567.37	287.82	10.49	638.21	1,795.81
Cachar	5.86	825.01	1,563.36	901.81	99.31	15.51	0	3,410.86
Assam	**240.34**	**5,972.5**	**15,989.8**	**13,603.2**	**5,204.02**	**2,963.11**	**2,031.28**	**46,004.2**

Source: Assam Gazettes 1947–2000.

District. Besides, land acquisition was also not high in the Karbi Anglong Hill District because it has only a small area that is prone to flood. The land acquisition, by and large, has been high in the flood-prone districts of the plains. The measure of embankment building, locally called *Mathauri*, has also been ineffective in controlling floods. It rather increased the intensity of the flood and siltation of the river bed. Ultimately, the sacrifice made by the people seems to have been largely wasted. And significantly, the government failed to achieve its objective of controlling the flood.

However, actual land acquisition under this category is much higher in quantum. By adding the land acquisition through the gazette notifications with other land transfers, Fernandes and Bharali (2000: 64) have estimated that actual land acquisition under this category stands at as high as 82,284.02 acres out of which 36,279.82 acres are CPRs.

Though the entire North East is known for its rich forests, national parks and wildlife sanctuaries, most of these forest lands did not have a formal area apart from Kaziranga and Manas national parks. Hence, the Government of Assam formally started acquiring land for these national parks and wildlife sanctuaries from 1979 till 2003. The national parks together occupied 1,52,846.07 acres of land. If we add this with two other existing national parks, that is, the famous Kaziranga National Park and Manas National Park, then it becomes 4,88,514.13 acres of area for all the national parks in Assam (Government of Assam 2003: 79). Table 3.5 shows that all the wildlife sanctuaries in Assam have occupied altogether 2,62,541.24 acres of forest lands (ibid.: 79). Now, if we add the area of all the national parks and wildlife sanctuaries of Assam together, they occupy a huge 7,51,055.37 acres of forest land. Additionally, the Government of Assam has declared two additional wildlife sanctuaries, that is, Deepar Beel adjacent to Guwahati and Bordoibaum in Dhemaji district, occupying 1,022.58 acres and 2,778.75 acres of land respectively. All this put together becomes a massive 7,54,856.7 acres of land. It must be pointed out that among all categories of development projects; land acquisition has been highest for the environment protection category.

TABLE 3.5
National Parks and Sanctuaries Started after 1947

National Parks and Sanctuaries	Districts	Area	Notification Year
(A) National Parks			
Nameri National Park	Sonitpur	49,400	1998
Dibru-Saikhowa National Park	Tinsukia/Dibrugarh	83,980	1999
Orang National Park	Darrang	19,466.07	1998
Total	**Assam**	**1,52,846.07**	
(B) Wild Life Sanctuaries			
Gibbon WLS	Jorhat	5,182.06	1997
Garampani WLS	Karbi Anglong	1,494.35	2002
Chakrasila WLS	Dhubri & Kokrajhar	11,255.79	1994
Burachapari WLS	Sonitpur	10,882.82	1995
Bornadi WLS	Darrang	6,476.34	1980
Pabitora WLS	Morigaon	9,583.6	1998
Panidihing WLS	Sibsagar	8,380.71	1995
Padumoni Bherjan Boajan WLS	Tinsukia	1,783.34	1999
East Karbi Anglong WLS	Karbi Anglong	54,787.07	2000
Laokhowa WLS	Nagaon	17,322.11	1979
Marat Langri WLS	Karbi Anglong	1,11,397	2003
Nambor-Doigurung WLS	Golaghat	23,996.05	2003
Total		**2,62,541.2**	
Grand Total (A+B)	**Assam**	**4,15,387.27**	

Source: Baruah 2002: 152–53.

Table 3.6 reflects an incomplete picture of the quantum of DPs as well as PAPs by a select number of environment protection-related projects from seven districts of Assam. The data shows that the number of DPs is very high, that is, 21,330, and the number of PAPs is also very high, that is, 91,536 persons. If we combine the DPs with the PAPs, the number becomes as high as 1,12,866 persons just for one category of development project. We have not been able to present the data of all the relevant projects for all the districts of Assam. Nevertheless, the data we have presented from the projects from select districts, though partial in nature, point to the enormity of the problem of DPs and PAPs. From this data one can very well guess the total number of IDPs generated in Assam by just one set of select development projects.

TABLE 3.6
DPs and PAPs of Representative Environment Projects 1947–2000

Project Code	District	DPs	PAPs	Total	Sources (File details)
Brahmaputra Dyke	Barpeta	473	7,882	8,355	Deputy Commissioner, Barpeta 1970I, 1973I, 1974D,1981O, 1986K
Kaldia Embankment	Barpeta	0	2,305	2,305	Deputy Commissioner, Barpeta 1976BI
Beki River Embankment	Barpeta	0	726	726	Deputy Commissioner, Barpeta 1966J, 1967B, 1968J, 1969O, 1981B
Chellengi River Embankment	Barpeta	17	1,155	1,172	Deputy Commissioner, Barpeta 1975D
Brahmaputra Dyke	Darrang	0	583	583	Executive Engineer, E & D, Darrang 1969A, B, 1998A, 1998B, 1998C, 1998J, 1998K, 1998L, 1998Q
Protection of Palasbari—Gumi from Erosion	Kamrup Rural	589	8,124	8,713	Deputy Commissioner, Kamrup (Rural) 1973I, 1984C, 1990B
Puthimari River Embankment	Kamrup Rural	1,914	4,983	6,897	Deputy Commissioner, Kamrup Rural 1960A, 1964F, 1968C, 1970CD
Baralia River Embankment	Kamrup Rural	649	616	1,265	Deputy Commissioner, Kamrup (Rural) 1960C
Pagladia Embankment	Kamrup Rural	512	72	584	Deputy Commissioner, Kamrup (Rural), 1964A, J
Noona Embankment	Kamrup Rural	176	154	330	Deputy Commissioner Kamrup (Rural) 1964A, 1964J, 1965F
Embankment on River Kopili	Karbi Anglong	33	1,276	1,309	Deputy Commissioner, Karbi Anglong 1976E
Subansiri Dyke	Lakhimpur	446	2,376	2,822	Deputy Commissioner, Lakhimpur 1983–84A, 1993–94A, 1990–01B, 1999–2000A
Brahmaputra Dyke	Lakhimpur	985	5,313	6,298	Deputy Commissioner, Lakhimpur 1996–97A, 1998–99A, B, C, D, 1999–2000A
Ranganadi Embankment	Lakhimpur	869	1,672	2,541	Deputy Commissioner, Lakhimpur, 1983–84H, 1986–87L, 1996–97B, 1998–99B

Dikrong Embankment	Lakhimpur	99	776	875	Deputy Commissioner, Lakhimpur, 1961A, 1978–79I, 1969–70B, 1981–82B, 1985–86A
Brahmaputra Dyke Bhajakhaity to Sonarigaon	Morigaon	1,188	4,015	5,203	Deputy Commissioner, Morigaon 1980N, 1980O, 1982A, 1982B
8th to 13th Km Bhuragaon Brahmaputra Dyke	Morigaon	3,504	5,858	9,362	Deputy Commissioner, Morigaon 1980N, 1980O, 1982A, 1982B
Gobha Dimoria Band at Kapili	Marigaon	600	3,817	4,417	Deputy Commissioner, Morigaon 1976J, 1976K, 1976L, 1976M
Brahmaputra Dyke from Dhing to Hiloikunda	Marigaon	1,920	11,385	13,305	Deputy Commissioner, Morigaon, 1968N, 1968O, 1968P & 1975I
Kallong Dyke from Raha to Jagi	Marigaon	28	1,034	1,062	Deputy Commissioner, Morigaon 1970G
Folong embankment	Marigaon	77	814	891	Deputy Commissioner, Morigaon 1980R
Kapili Tributary Dyke	Marigaon	325	1,100	1,425	Deputy Commissioner, Morigaon 1969G, 1969H, 1975S
Silaghat to Hiloikhunda B/dyke	Marigaon	1,288	6,188	7,476	Deputy Commissioner, Morigaon 1987S
Brahmaputra Dyke	Marigaon	341	1,843	2,184	Deputy Commissioner, Morigaon 1982C, 1985A, 1992X, 1992W
Barnodi Embankment	Nalbari	479	611	1,090	Deputy Commissioner, Nalbari 1970I
Embankment Pagaldia	Nalbari	4,466	14,779	19,245	Deputy Commissioner, Nalbari 1960A, 1980B, 1990P
Brahmaputra Embankment	Nalbari	352	2,079	2,431	Deputy Commissioner, Nalbari 1968L, 1969X, 1969W, 1969A, 1969J
Total		**21,330**	**91,536**	**1,12,866**	

Source: Government of Assam.

D. Transport and Communication

Under this category, the Government of Assam acquired 28,617.17 acres of land in total through the gazette notifications from time to time. This category includes the land acquisition for roads, railways, airports, etc., besides post and telegraph and other projects.

The transport and communication system in Assam remained precarious during the colonial period. It was worse in other North Eastern states and the entire hill areas. Partition of India in 1947, following independence, further constricted the transport and communication network. During the post-colonial period, attempts were made slowly in Assam or for that matter in the entire North East to improve the transport and communication network as a part of development of basic infrastructure. From Table 3.7, it is found that during the period of 1961–70, land acquisition has been the highest. During this period, because of strategic compulsions, the government went in for massive acquisition of land for transport and communication. However, we must note that the data presented in Table 3.7 does in no way reflect the exact situation of land acquisition in Assam. What we have presented here is from the government gazette notifications only. It represents a part of the total situation. In a recent study, Fernandes and Bharali (2006: 65–67) have used other reasonably reliable sources to extrapolate, on the basis of which they have found that a much larger quantum of land acquisition under the category of transport and communication had taken place in Assam—1,15,288.14 acres of land as against 28,617.17 acres shown in the gazette notifications. The extent of land acquired according to extrapolated data is more than four times higher than the officially available data in the gazettes.

Table 3.8 shows the number of DPs and PAPs generated by a set of representative transport and communication projects in Assam. The new acquisition of 4,303.03 acres of land for railways induced displacement of 5,141 DPs and 7,474 PAPs; in total 12,615 persons. For a select section of the National Highway, the government acquired an additional 1,512 acres of land, which induced 2,361 DPs and 1,347 PAPs, totalling 3,708 persons. For upgrading two existing airports, the government acquired additional 252.42 acres of land and generated

TABLE 3.7
Decade-wise Land Acquisition for Transport and Communication 1947–2000

Districts	1947–50	1951–60	1961–70	1971–80	1981–90	1991–2000	NA	Total
Dhubri	59.88	351.05	297.67	13.24	417.39	70.78	19.23	1,229.24
Kokrajhar	666.56	932.93	898.4	299.97	23.28	8.24		2,829.38
Bongaigaon	45.45	10.98	234.19	20.21	19.29	57.92	201.98	590.02
Goalpara	58.62	331.8	179.35	738.41	568.29	110.55	0.07	1,987.09
Barpeta	12.17	1.81	230.38	223.64	58.24	10.88	4.21	541.33
Nalbari	34	474.6	40.18	24.7	20.1	29.4	38.65	661.63
Kamrup	48.52	542.41	1,188.57	201.63	1,350.9	61.47	55.3	3,448.8
Darrang	14.87	57.47	60.22	70.98	41.95	7.8		253.29
Sonitpur	115.18	306.55	1,578.67	191.88	179.21	3	9.84	2,384.33
Lakhimpur	10.77	1,408	1,408.37	176.08	10.41	19.09		3,032.72
Dhemaji	0	0	567.9	69.73	16.46	0		654.09
Morigaon	11.41	49	1.93	1.48	2.97	222.4	5.31	294.5
Nagaon	144.77	56.86	5.8	87.82	83	0.58		378.83
Golaghat	77.53	64.25	55.86	33.57	33.31	78.1	12.11	354.73
Jorhat	23.07	182.7	77.02	22.57	34.81	2.64		342.81
Sibsagar	72.72	246.02	246.02	87.13	248.06	183.3	27.7	1,110.95
Dibrugarh	2,202	130.34	158.08	7.13	77.68	0		2,575.23
Tinsukia	0.27	9.84	25.29	14.64	19.33	0	52.2	121.57
Karbi Anglong	2.12	0	2.12	13.42	63.2	218.61	0.92	300.39
N.C. Hills	2.35	0	5.31	0	0	853.08		860.74
Karimganj	4.69	182.45	738.81	244.42	108.88	118.74	43.28	1,441.27
Hailakandi	2.24	53.35	100.77	60.45	679.58	225.48	0.52	1,122.39
Cachar	4.92	632.66	460.95	157.74	782.71	62.86		2,101.84
Assam	**3,614.11**	**6,025.07**	**8,561.86**	**2,760.84**	**4,839.05**	**2,344.92**	**471.32**	**28,617.17**

Source: Assam Gazettes 1947–2000.

TABLE 3.8

DPs and PAPs of Representative Transport and Communication Projects 1947–2000

Project Code	District	DPs	PAPs	Total	Land	Sources (File details)
BG Rly Line	Kamrup (Urban)	61	420	481	600.00	Deputy Commissioner, Kamrup (Urban) 1981M, 1981N, 1985F
BG Rly Line	Kamrup (Rural)	644	1,204	1,848	1,070.32	Deputy Commissioner Kamrup (Rural) 1986I, 1987M, 1988L, 1988N, 1988O, 1995G
BG Rly Line	Goalpara	2,163	5,325	7,488	1,122.71	Deputy Commissioner, Goalpara 1987T, 1988IO, 1989A, 1990AB, 1991R, 1992A, 1992G
Kapili River Bridge	Morigaon	138	194	332	450.00	Deputy Commissioner, Morigaon. 1968I, 1968J, 1968K, 1975P, 1976H
Bogibeel Bridge	Dhemaji, Dibrugarh	1,975	200	2,175	800.00	Deputy Commsissioner, Dhemaji 2000A, Deputy Commissioner, Dibrugarh 2002U
Rly Crossing Bridge	Kamrup (Urban)	160	131	291	260.00	Deputy Commissioner, Kamrup (Urban) 1963B, 1963C
Total Railways		**5,141**	**7,474**	**12,615**	**4,303.03**	
NH 37	Kamrup (Urban)	154	132	286	185	Deputy Commissioner, Kamrup (Urban) 1963A, 1963G
NH 31	Nalbari	1,414	728	2,142	1,007	Deputy Commissioner, Kamrup 1963A, DC, Nalbari 1960N, 1969AE, 1965H, 1970R
NH 39	Golaghat	44	39	83	65	Deputy Commissioner, Golaghat 1969I, 1980D, 1999A
NH 36	Karbi Anglong	215	126	341	95	Deputy Commissioner, Karbi Anglong 1981G, 1984A,C, 1986D,I, 1987M, 1988B, 1989A, 1989D, 1989H, 1989G, 1989J, 1989M, 1990A
NH 31	Kamrup (Rural)	253	191	444	110	Deputy Commissioner, Kamrup (Rural) 1964E, 1972E

Exp. NH Narengi-Khanapara	Kamrup (Urban)	281	131	412	50	Deputy Commissioner, Kamrup (Urban) 1964A, 1986H,D, 1989C, 1993C
Total for NH		**2,361**	**1,347**	**3,708**	**1,512**	
Hatigaon-Namghar	Kamrup (Urban)	8	20	28	20	Deputy Commissioner, Kamrup (Urban) 1987 A
Jagiroad-Dangabari	Marigaon	17	10	27	13.72	Deputy Commissioner, Morigaon. 1975G, 1975H, 1975I
KB Road	Cachar	0	18	18	19	Deputy Commissioner, Cachar 1956G, 1956F
Total Other Roads		**25**	**48**	**73**	**52.72**	
Tel. Exchange	Kamrup (Urban)	20	30	50	46.16	Deputy Commissioner, Kamrup (Urban) 1972A
Fuleral Post Office	Cachar	2	6	8	14.92	Deputy Commissioner, Cachar 1976F
Total Others		**22**	**36**	**58**	**61.08**	
Borjhar Airport	Kamrup (Rural)	303	650	953	143.62	Deputy Commissioner, Kamrup (Rural) 1990E, 1996C, 2000E, 2000F, 2000H
Mohanbari Airport	Dibrugarh	22	300	322	108.8	Deputy Commissioner, Dibrugarh 1999A
Total Airports		**325**	**950**	**1,275**	**252.42**	

Source: Government of Assam.

TABLE 3.9

DPs and PAPs of Transport and Communication Projects 1947–2000

Project	DPs	PAPs	Tribals	Per cent	Others	Per cent	NA	Per cent	Total
Highway	31,985	18,248	188	0.47	325	0.81	49,720	98.72	50,233
PWD	32,148	62,244	341	0.53	3,593	1.28	63,106	98.19	94,392
Airports	488	1,424	25	1.31	297	15.53	1,590	83.16	1,912
Post-Telegraph	1,283	2,942	NA	NA	NA	NA	4,225	100	4,225
Total	**65,904**	**84,858**	**554**	**0.5**	**4,215**	**1.22**	**1,18,641**	**98.19**	**1,50,762**

Source: Fernandes and Bharali 2006: 98.

325 DPs and 950 PAPs, totalling to 1,275 persons. Table 3.8 shows a partial picture, the actual number of DPs and PAPs generated by the transport and communication projects is obviously much higher.

Table 3.9 has shown the number of DPs and PAPs of transport and communication projects in Assam. Through extrapolation, Fernandes and Bharali (2006) have estimated the total number of DPs and PAPs induced by these projects respectively at 65,904 persons and 84,858 persons. Hence, the grand total becomes 1,50,762 persons.

Now, again it has been realized that transport and communication of the North East is crucial for the region's internal development, its linkages with the rest of India, and India's strategic interests. Besides, the Government of India is exploring the possibility of opening up the North East with South East Asia as a part of the much hyped Look East Policy. Hence, the Government of Assam has issued notifications to acquire large tracts of land to expand the National Highway passing through Assam as a part of the East–West corridor. The Asian Highway project is likely to cover a large part of the North Eastern states. Thus, this decade will see more acquisition of land for the transport and communication category. This infrastructure building project is likely to accentuate the problem of displacement further in Assam and other North Eastern states.

E. Water Resource Projects

Water resource projects include irrigation, hydroelectric dams, canals and their infrastructural facilities. Table 3.10 presents information on the quantum of land acquisition in Assam for the water resource projects during 1947–2000. During the post-colonial period, Assam started a large number of water resource projects throughout the state. It was assumed that the water resource projects would boost the agricultural productivity and the much needed electric supply for the underdeveloped state. However, the actual story is quite different.

As per the Assam government's gazette notification during the period 1947 to 2000, it acquired 27,333.37 acres of land for various water resource projects. Table 3.10 also shows the high degree of unevenness in land acquisition among the districts. The government

TABLE 3.10

Land Acquisition for Water Resource Projects by District 1947–2000

District	1947–50	1951–60	1961–70	1971–80	1981–90	1991–2000	NA	Total
Cachar	0	0	4.41	40.61	6.63	0	0	51.65
Dhubri	0	0	0	80.03	314.31	9.98	96.56	500.88
Kokrajhar	40.52	3.49	212.12	410.68	269.98	60.83	0	997.62
Bongaigaon	0	35.16	10.52	22.24	0	1.65	124.39	193.96
Goalpara	0	14.21	68.86	3.61	101.84	11.74	0	200.26
Barpeta	0.91	0	124.81	796.71	416.94	21.02	6.12	1,366.51
Nalbari	9.06	317.43	59.45	480.12	403.77	28.66	2,215.93	3,514.42
Kamrup	0.31	23.27	58.81	815.8	95.1	0	132.92	1,126.21
Darrang	0	9.19	138.3	510.41	503.3	146.3	0.12	1,307.62
Sonitpur	0	228.85	406.01	483.36	267.3	0	53.1	1,438.62
Lakhimpur	0	0	90.21	9.93	25.07	96.03	0	221.24
Dhemaji	0	0	0.51	5.39	60.17	3.76	37.06	106.89
Morigaon	0	0	20.6		1.5	0	213.48	235.58
Nagaon	1.56	0	653.81	2,093.69	348.14	4.04	0	3,101.24
Golaghat	0	0	50.86	23.41	9.51	0.02	0.68	84.48
Jorhat	0	49.29	178.57	0.53	11.64	0.62	0	240.65
Sibsagar	51.85	25.62	22.19	161.57	17.79	4.21	81.75	364.98
Dibrugarh	0	0	5.08	73.7	208.06	2.39	0	289.23
Tinsukia	0	0	0	3.19	0	0	0	3.19
K Anglong	0	0	272.1	441.89	187.64	5.21	884.46	1,791.3
N.C. Hills	0	0	16.12	216.47	2,445.3	7,324.44	0	10,002.33
Karimganj	0	9.93	0	141.52	29.61	1.29	12.16	194.51
Total	**104.21**	**716.44**	**2,393.34**	**6,814.86**	**5,723.6**	**7,722.19**	**3,858.73**	**27,333.37**

Source: Assam Gazettes 1947–2000.

acquired 10,002.33 acres of land from North Cachar Hill District alone and only 3.19 acres of land from Tinsukia district. However, the actual quantum of land acquisition is much larger than what has been demonstrated in the Table because this Table includes only the land acquisition related information that appeared in the government gazette notifications. The actual quantum of land acquisition has been massive for the water resource projects in Assam, though most of the projects have ultimately failed to reach their targets and there has been enormous wastage of public money.

We have already noted the inadequacy of data on land acquisition for the water resource projects. Through extrapolation from different reliable sources, Fernandes and Bharali (2006: 44–54) have demonstrated that the actual land acquisition under this category is several times higher than what has been shown in the government gazette notifications. This is evident from Table 3.11. According to them, massive 1,91,308.15 acres of land was acquired for the water resource projects in Assam. Besides, Table 3.11 clearly reflects the type of land acquired by the government, that is, private and CPRs. The gazette notifications included only a portion of private land, not all the private land. It totally excludes the land acquired from CPRs. For example, the government acquired 41,835.34 acres of land from private ownership and 84,938.42 acres from CPRs which constitute 21 per cent for the category of private ownership and remaining 44 per cent under the CPRs category, respectively. The acquisition of CPRs land has remained somewhat invisible. Hence, one can safely assume that the government's land acquisition for water resource projects included a substantial chunk of CPR land. This mainly affected the tribal

TABLE 3.11
**Type of Land Used by Major, Medium and Minor Water
Resource Projects (in acres) 1947–2000**

Category	Private	Per cent	CPRs	Per cent	NA	Per cent	Total
Major	27,970.45	33	56,788.48	67	00.00	00.00	84,758.93
Medium	13,864.89	33	28,149.94	67	00.00	00.00	42,014.83
Minor	NA	NA	NA	NA	64,534.39	100.00	64,534.39
Total	**41,835.34**	**21.87**	**84,938.42**	**44.40**	**64,534.39**	**33.73**	**1,91,308.15**

Source: Fernandes and Bharali 2006: 54.

people who have been using the land belonging to the CPR category for their sustenance.

Table 3.12 shows the number of DPs and PAPs during the period 1947 to 2000 caused by the water resource projects in Assam. Three categories of water resource projects together induced massive displacement of population in Assam. It has been found that these water resource projects alone have induced 49,977 DPs and 3,98,835 PAPs (Fernandes and Bharali 2006: 86).

The quantum of irrigated land in Assam is low compared to the all-India average. Most of its agriculture is still dependent on the vagaries of nature. Notwithstanding all this, water resource projects initiated by the government have induced 4,48,812 DPs and PAPs.

F. Industry

Development and more specifically industrial development became the major concern of all the newly liberated nation-states of the South. It was regarded as an instrument for building the new post-colonial nation-state. India too vigorously attempted this. In the process, new industrial estates, growth centres and industrial areas were developed under the aegis of the state to give a boost to India's endeavour for industrial development. Assam too embarked on the same industrial projects.

Table 3.13 shows the quantum of land acquisition in Assam during the post-colonial period beginning from 1951 to 2000 for establishing industrial estates, growth centres and industrial areas. This list is selective not exhaustive and hence it provides a partial picture. Significantly, it shows zero land acquisition for the Lakhimpur, Dhemaji, Darrang and North Cachar Hill districts. All these districts have remained absolutely underdeveloped in terms of industrial growth. Land acquisition has been highest in the Sibsagar district followed by the Kamrup district. Consequently, one can see the uneven growth of industries in an industrially underdeveloped state. According to gazette notifications, the Government of Assam acquired 7,141.13 acres of land. However, this does not reflect the real situation. It is much more different than what has been shown. Actual land acquisition has been much higher than what has been shown in Table 3.13.

TABLE 3.12
Estimates of DPs and PAPs Caused by Water Resource Projects 1947–2000

Category	DPs	Per cent	PAPs	Per cent	Tribe	Per cent	Others	Per cent	NA	Per cent	Total
Major	27,236	51.66	25,489	48.34	17,285	32.17	20,150	38.83	15,290	29.00	52,725
Medium	5,707	34.09	11,034	65.91	7,729	46.17	4,911	29.34	4,101	25.00	16,741
Minor	17,034	4.49	3,62,312	95.51	1,32,772	35	2,46,574	65	00	00.0	3,79,346
Total	**49,977**	**11.14**	**3,98,835**	**88.86**	**1,57,786**	**35.16**	**2,71,635**	**60.52**	**19,391**	**4.32**	**4,48,812**

Source: Fernandes and Bharali 2006: 86.

TABLE 3.13

Land Used by Selected Industrial Estates, Growth Centres, Industrial Areas and Others 1951–2000

Districts	1951–60	1961–70	1971–80	1981–90	1991–2000	NA	Total
Dhubri	3.42	6.29	0.9	0.82	0	0	11.43
Kokrajhar	0	200.91	2.09	0	47.55	0	250.55
Bongaigaon	0	0	12.25	0.42	4.98	4.98	22.63
Goalpara	0	0	0.69	0	2.72	0	3.41
Barpeta	9.18	133.02	334	12	0	0.41	488.61
Nalbari	0	114.63	3.36	10.29	0	0	128.28
Kamrup	52.37	636.24	352.42	25.82	2.85	108.22	1,177.92
Darrang	0	0	0	0	0		0
Dibrugarh	0	155.27	334.5	0	4.66	0.19	494.62
Sonitpur	0	0	0	7.05	0	0	7.05
Lakhimpur	0	0	0	0	0	0	0
Dhemaji	0	0	0	0	0	0	0
Morigaon	0	117.41	2.86	200.74	7.32	0.54	328.87
Nagaon	0	341.51	25.45	6.67	1.86	0	375.49
Golaghat	40.18	274.78	3.17	0.81	0	462.33	781.27
Jorhat	0	120.88	0.08	28.99	0	106.19	256.14
Sibsagar	0	202.72	206.07	447.08	132.29	602.61	1,590.77
Dibrugarh	0	155.27	334.5	0	4.66	0.19	494.62
Tinsukia	0	1.04	1.57	0	0	0	2.61
K Anglong	0	0	0	1.45	0	0	1.45
N.C. Hills	0	0	0	0	0	0	0
Karimganj	0	0	4.19	116.85	30.96	65.59	217.59
Hailakandi	0	0	0	45.12	14.55	55.45	115.12
Cachar	0	8.32	0	0	303.87	80.51	392.7
Assam	**105.15**	**2,468.29**	**1,618.1**	**904.11**	**558.27**	**1,487.21**	**7,141.13**

Source: Assam Gazettes 1951–2000.

Table 3.14 shows the quantum of land acquisition for selected industries. The major industries have taken over a large chunk of land. This is in addition to what has been shown in the previous Table. The major industries have been divided into two categories; those which acquired more than 1,000 acres and those which acquired less than that. The major categories here are composed of Nagaon Paper Mills, Noonmati Refinery, Bongaigaon Refinery and Petrochemical Complex, and Panchgram Paper Mills. The government acquired 12,500 acres of land for these major industries. Additionally, the government acquired in total 1,546 acres of land for Numaligarh Refinery Limited, Cachar Sugar Mill and Assam State Fertilizer Company. For the selected seven medium industries, the government acquired another 502.83 acres of land. In total, all these selected industries acquired 14,548.83 acres of land. Again this is not the whole story. It narrates only a portion of the story of land acquisition because it does not include all the industries of Assam.

As per government information, Assam has 21 major industries and 97 medium industries in different sectors in different districts outside the government sponsored Industrial Estates (Government of Assam 2004–05). By extrapolating the number of industries and the rate of land acquisition per category of industries, Fernandes and Bharali (2006: 57) have come to the conclusion that the government of Assam acquired 31,410.19 acres of land for various industrial projects, as evident from Table 3.15. Obviously such huge land acquisition led to the generation of a large number of DPs and PAPs. This has happened because the government chose to acquire a major chunk of land from the CPRs category.

Table 3.16 shows that major large industries induced 4,860 DPs and 4,062 PAPs, large-scale industries induced 6,761 DPs and 11,956 PAPs, medium-scale industries induced 1,530 DPs and 19,584 PAPs and industrial infrastructure building induced 1,069 DPs and 7,910 PAPs in Assam. In total, industries induced 14,220 DPs and 43,512 PAPs in Assam. Hence, put together, land acquisition for industries induced 57,732 DPs and PAPs. Very significantly, land acquisition for industrial projects affected the tribal people deeply. The share of tribals among the DPs and PAPs is as high as 78 per cent for the category of major large industries and 68 per cent for the medium-scale

TABLE 3.14

Land Used for Some Selected Industries (in acres) 1950–2000

Projects			Land used			
Major Industries	Districts	Private	Common	Total	Sources	
Nagaon Paper Mill	Morigaon	1,200	300	1,500	PRO, NPM 2005	
Noonmati Refinery	Kamrup	603	3,397	4,000	Deputy Commissioner Kamrup (Urban) 1960E, F, 1963N and Gazettes 1947–2000	
BRPL	Bongaigaon	565	5,435	6,000	Deputy Commissioner Bongaigaon 1973A, 1979A	
Panchgram Paper Mill	Hailakandi	550	450	1,000	Bhattacharjee 2003: 47–48	
Total		**2,918**	**9,582**	**12,500**		
Numaligarh Refinery	Golaghat	269	481	750	Baruah 1999: 20	
Cachar Sugar Mill	Cachar	513	0	513	Gazettes 1947–2000	
Assam State Fertilizer	Kamrup	0	283	283	Knowledgeable Person 2005L	
Total		**782**	**764**	**1,546**		
Medium Industries						
Assam Hard Board Ltd	Kamrup	100	110	210	Knowledgeable Person 2005J	
National Textile Corpn	Kamrup	0	12	12	PRO NTCL 2005	
Ashok Paper Mill	Bongaigaon	9.83	28	37.83	PCCF 2005	
Fertichem Ltd	Kamrup	0	8	8	Knowledgeable Person 2005G	
Assam Advastas Ltd	Kamrup	17	0	17	Knowledgeable Person 2005M	
LPG Bottling Plant	Kamrup	148	0	148	Deputy Commissioner Kamrup 1991T, 1994B	
Assam Cotton Mills	Sonitpur	0	70	70	Knowledgeable Person 2005E	
Total		**274.83**	**228**	**502.83**		

Grand Total Land Acquisition: 14,548.83 acres.

Table 3.15
Type of Land Acquired for Industrial Projects 1947–2000

Category	Private Land	Per cent	Common Property Resources	Per cent	Total	Percentage of Total
Major Large-scale	2,918	23	9,582	77	12,500	40
Large-scale	4,170.49	51	4,074.84	49	8,245.33	26
Medium-scale	3,345.19	55	2,774.81	45	6,120	20
Other Industrial Projects	106.89	4	2,496.63	96	2,603.52	8
Pipelines	776.74	40	1,164.6	60	1,941.34	6
Total	**11,317.31**	**36.03**	**20,092.88**	**63.97**	**31,410.19**	**100**

Source: Fernandes and Bharali: 2006.

TABLE 3.16
Industry-wise DPs and PAPs in Assam 1947–2000

Type	DPs	PAPs	Tribal	Per cent	Others	Per cent	NA	Per cent	Total
Major									
Large-scale	4,860	4,062	6,961	78.01	1,961	21.99	00	00	8,922
Large-scale	6,761	11,956	10,482	56.00	8,235	44.00	00	00	18,717
Medium-scale	1,530	19,584	12,668	68.00	8,446	40.00	00	00	21,114
Infrastructure	1,069	7,910	1,500	16.71	4,476	83.29	3,003		8,979
Total	**14,220**	**43,512**	**31,611**		**23,118**		**3,003**		**57,732**

Source: Fernandes and Bharali 2006.

industries. This has happened because the government went in for massive acquisition of land under CPRs and that has directly affected the tribal people severely.

G. Enormity of Land Acquisition

We have already shown a few project-wise situations of land acquisition in Assam and its consequent number of DPs and PAPs. Instead of going for all the land acquisition for all the government-sponsored development projects individually, we would now prefer to take up all the projects collectively for the analysis of land acquisition. Of course, we have already shown the quantum of land acquisition for the select major development projects. Now, it would be of crucial importance to understand the quantum of land acquisition in its totality by including all other projects in a nutshell which we did not take into account in our earlier discussion.

Table 3.17 enumerates the total amount of land acquisition, that is, 3,92,597.55 acres of land for all the state-sponsored development projects for the entire state of Assam during 1947 to 2000. In terms of individual category, the government acquired the largest amount of land for the category of administration. As per gazette notifications, the government acquired a huge 2,25,562.66 acres of land for administration during the period 1947–2000. These lands were used to build mainly government offices and residential quarters for its employees. During the entire post-colonial period, Assam witnessed an unprecedented expansion of government machinery and administration. Administrative units multiplied manifold. The number of districts increased from 6 in 1940 to 10 in 1970, 23 in 1990 to 27 in 2005. These 27 districts have 45 sub-divisions, 134 revenue circles and 131 community development blocks in all. Some of the old single districts have become five districts over a period of time. For example, the old Goalpara district has now become five districts, that is, Goalpara, Dhubri, Bongaigaon, Kokrajhar and Chirang. Very similar are the cases of old Kamrup and Lakhimpur districts. Such multiplication of districts and sub-divisions have led to the expansion of government establishments for offices and residences. All this contributed towards the high quantum of land acquisition during 1947–2000. That is not the end, there is the likelihood of further increase in the number of districts in the wake of acceptance of autonomous councils for tribal people living in the plains of Assam. Consequently, one can expect more displacement of population and its resultant demand for resettlement and rehabilitation.

Table 3.17 demonstrates that the water resource projects acquired 27,333.37 acres of land. Similarly, land acquisition for environment protection, and transport and communication was 46,004.2 acres and 28,617.17 acres respectively. Besides, the government also acquired land for various other development projects like mines, non-hydel projects, human resource development projects, farms and fisheries, urban development, housing, social welfare, tourism, health and other minor projects. All these acquisitions took place through gazette notifications. These show an enormous amount of land acquisition in Assam; 3,92,597.55 acres of land for different categories of development projects in the state.

TABLE 3.17

Decade-wise Total Land Acquired for Different Projects Under Gazette Notifications 1947–2000

Projects	1947–50	1951–60	1961–70	1971–80	1981–90	1991–2000	NA	Total
Water Resources	104.21	716.44	2,393.34	6,814.86	5,723.6	7,722.19	3,858.73	27,333.37
Industry	0	105.16	2,468.29	1,618.1	904.11	558.27	1,487.21	7,141.14
Mines	–	3.47	11.15	–	–	0.9	2.91	18.43
Non-hydel Power	0	8.89	583.89	93.92	234.2	2.16	38.97	962.03
Defence and Security	6.69	790.63	5,135.69	2,009.37	678.56	289.06	181.4	9,091.4
Environment and Protection	240.34	5,972.5	15,989.8	13,603.2	5,204.02	2,963.11	2,031.28	46,004.25
Transport and Communication	3,614.11	6,025.07	8,561.86	2,760.84	4,839.05	2,344.92	471.32	28,617.17
Human Resource Development	55.01	225.76	105.78	25.84	32.32	53.7	24.18	522.59
Refugee Resettlement	3,305.24	12,068.82	531.73	379.81	2.15	4.76	5.39	16,297.9
Farms and Fisheries	284.16	593.44	251.37	58.76	17.49	7.48	171.24	1,383.94
Urban Development	593.26	478.16	92.62	19.85	3.53	5.91	0	1,193.33
Housing	1,113.07	323.42	278.03	336.42	345.85	310.02	30.91	2,737.72
Social Welfare	48.86	5,833.02	8,875.6	2,442.52	32.48	0.36	21.46	17,254.3
Tourism	–	2.22	0.53	–	–	–	5.14	7.89
Health	76.75	327.27	269.34	68.67	108.95	37.53	0	888.51
Education	301.89	695.77	1,307.08	19.12	150.45	29.14	1,125.96	3,629.41
Administration	834.65	40,285.72	54,428.11	83,026.75	40,849.61	6,094.03	43.79	2,25,562.66
Others	4.94	1,882.47	1,443.42	574.97	45.32	–	0.39	3,951.51
Total	**10,583.18**	**76,338.23**	**1,02,727.63**	**1,13,853**	**59,171.69**	**20,423.54**	**9,500.28**	**3,92,597.55**

Source: Assam Gazettes 1947–2000.

However, Table 3.18 shows a much larger amount of land acquisition than Table 3.17. The data for Table 3.17 was collected from the Assam Gazettes while the data for Table 3.18 has been extrapolated from different reliable sources. If we make a decadal comparison, we find that during the decade 1971–80, land acquisition was highest in Assam.

From the data that we have shown in Table 3.18, it is possible to draw the conclusion that the land acquisition during the postcolonial period for the state of Assam has been extremely high for different categories of development projects. As per gazette notifications, the Government of Assam acquired in total 3,92,597.45 acres of land but the actual acquisition was more than three times higher, at 14,01,184.77 acres of land. This amounts to 8 per cent of Assam's total land. Such a massive land acquisition is bound to induce displacement of population and increase the quantum of PAPs in the state. Obviously, that affected a large number of people in Assam. Many affected people say that the government acquired more land than was required. What is more important to note here is that in the wake of globalization of Indian economy, a large tract of land ostensibly acquired in 'public interest' is likely to be transferred to private sector establishments. It must be noted that as the government is handing over many of its establishments to the private sector, most of these precious lands are likely to be transferred to powerful private owners.

H. Quantum of Displacement

The quantum of land acquisition has given us an overall view about the internal displacement of population within the state of Assam caused by various state-sponsored development projects. We have already seen that the state was involved in land acquisition for different public purposes. Quantitatively, the land acquisition has been massive if we look into the size of the state and the land–man ratio. The land–man ratio has become adverse over the years. At one stage, the land–man ratio in Assam was better than the all-India average. As per the 2001 Census, the land–man ratio in Assam had gone up to 340 as against the all-India ratio of 324 persons per square kilometre.

TABLE 3.18
Total Land Acquired for Different Projects: Gazettes and Calculation 1947–2000

Projects	Gazettes	Per cent	CPRs	Per cent	NA	Per cent	Total
Water Resources	41,835.34	21.87	84,938.42	44.4	64,534.39	33.73	1,91,308.15
Industry	11,317.31	36.03	20,092.88	63.97	0	0	31,410.19
Mines	105.47	0.37	7,894.53	28.05	20,145	71.58	28,145.00
Non-hydro Power	2,187.17	19.94	8,781.29	80.06	0	0	10,968.46
Defence and Security	9,483.03	35.91	1,988.04	7.53	14,933.44	56.56	26,404.51
Environment Protection	46,002.2	55.91	36,279.82	44.09	0	0	82,282.02
Transport and Communication	7,054.36	6.10	11,999.41	10.39	96,459.05	83.51	1,15,512.82
Farms/Fisheries	1,383.94	0.57	2,27,269.2	94.99	10,597.3	4.42	2,39,250.48
Refugees	16,297	4.65	3,33,703	95.34	0	0	3,50,000.00
Social Welfare	17,254.3	99.75	42.44	0.25	0	0	17,296.74
HRD	647.77	35.68	1,167.89	64.32	0	0	1,815.66
Urban	1,193.33	100	0	0	0	0	1,193.33
Education	2,464	10.43	500	2.17	20,656	87.45	23,620.00
Health	3,400	56.12	2,658	43.88	0	0	6,058.00
Administration	2,25,562.7	83.89	43,307.96	16.11	0	0	2,68,870.62
Others	7,048.79	100	0	0	0	0	7,048.79
Total	**3,92,597.45**	–	**7,80,622**	–	**2,27,325**	–	**14,01,184.77**

Source: Gazettes of Assam 1947–2000 and Fernandes and Bharali 2006: 185.

However, the actual picture is worse if we look into the land–man ratio in the two valleys of Assam, that is, the Brahmaputra and the Barak valley. For the Brahmaputra valley, it is as high as 407 persons and for the Barak valley, as high as 448 persons per square kilometre. These ratios are much higher than the national average. As per the 2001 Census, the land–man ratio in Assam's two hill districts is only 58 persons per square kilometre. The low density of population in Assam's hill district has substantially neutralized the land–man ratio of the state. Nevertheless, the density of population in Assam's plains today is comparable to any high density region of India. In other words, the per capita availability of land has shrunk substantially over the years. In the absence of industrial development, the pressure on agricultural land has augmented adversely.

It would be important to recollect here that during the colonial period upto 1947, tea gardens in Assam occupied 4,50,000 acres of land in the plains (Sharma 1999). The colonial state very generously allotted/leased out land to the tea planters, mostly the British. Very significantly, the amount of land under the tea gardens increased further to 6,61,960 acres during the post-colonial period (Government of Assam 2003). Officially, tea gardens are isolated enclaves still known as 'estates'. If we exclude the innumerable rivers, particularly the very wide Brahmaputra, the land occupied by the tea gardens and land acquired for all the development projects, the actual land–man ratio becomes more adverse indeed than what is apparent. The hard fact is that Assam is no longer a land-abundant state, it has transformed into a high density state in terms of population wherein land is increasingly becoming a scarce commodity. Landholdings are becoming smaller and a large number of poor people are losing their land as a consequence of land acquisition by the state for various development projects.

Table 3.19 shows project-wise number of displaced persons in Assam as per information from government sources. Table 3.19 shows that 38,438 persons were displaced by various development projects in Assam. A significant number of them belong to the scheduled castes and scheduled tribes category. However, we feel it is an underestimation of the total number of displaced persons. This data includes only the people who received some compensation for their

TABLE 3.19
Project-wise Number of Displaced Persons in Assam 1947–2000

Projects	SC	ST	MOBC	GEN	NA	Total
Water Project	66	264	0	55	1,254	1,639
Industry	28	110	0	55	83	276
Mines	0	0	0	5	0	5
NHD	0	0	0	28	0	28
Defence	182	33	0	330	589	1,134
Environment	138	66	17	380	22,803	23,404
Transport	28	308	83	352	8,905	9,676
HRD	0	0	0	33	0	33
Refugee	0	0	0	6	0	6
Farms	0	0	0	0	215	215
Urban Development	0	0	0	55	17	72
Housing	83	0	0	11	6	100
Social Welfare	0	0	0	0	0	0
Tourism	0	0	0	0	0	0
Health	0	0	0	0	429	429
Education	28	0	0	0	1,095	1,123
Administration	6	11	0	22	259	298
Total	**559**	**792**	**100**	**1,332**	**35,655**	**38,438**

Source: Offices of the Deputy Commissioners, Districts of Assam.

land from the government. The people who were displaced from government land, and forest dwellers who did not have legally valid land documents like *patta*, and those who did not receive any monetary compensation from the Government of Assam, were not included under the purview of displaced persons. Contrary to hard empirical reality, the government does not recognize them as displaced persons. Consequently, the government itself underestimated the number of displaced persons in Assam. Obviously, it helped the government to minimize its cost of compensation.

Development projects in Assam not only displaced people physically from their home and land, but also had direct bearing on their income and livelihood. Displacement, if not backed up by a concerted resettlement and rehabilitation support, can accentuate their impoverishment risks. Table 3.20 demonstrates that a massive 51,437 families in Assam lost their livelihood as a result of development-induced displacement. However, if we assume that each family on an average consists of five members, then the number

TABLE 3.20
Number of Families Deprived of their Livelihood by Development Projects 1947–2000

Projects	NA	1940–50	1951–60	1961–70	1971–80	1981–90	1991–2000	2000+	Total
Water Resources	4,618	0	0	314	5,442	2,267	497	54	13,192
Industry	360	0	236	142	23	98	322	0	1,181
Mines	43	0	0				20	0	63
Non-hydel Power	0	0	0	24	16	36	5	0	81
Defence and Security	81	0	193	728	900	324	27	0	2,253
Environment and Protection	11,329	0	1,401	3,229	2,244	2,022	928	224	21,377
Transport and Communication	2,619	5	630	1,801	1,174	1,606	1,388	35	9,258
Human Resource Development	63	0	172	175	0	55	13	0	478
Refugee Resettlement	0	29	562	0	15	0	0	0	606
Farms and Fisheries	2	0	48	76	5	1	0	0	132
Urban Development	14	0	5	15	0	42	43	0	119
Housing	12	0	4	31	29	0	10	0	86
Social Welfare	0	0	57	33	0	0	0	0	90
Tourism	10	0	0	0	0	0	0	0	10
Health	46	0	9	499	42	544	66	400	1,606
Education	92	0	26	71	12	159	49	7	416
Govt. Offices	137	0	32	30	126	114	13	0	452
Others	0	0	8	2	3	24	0	0	37
Total	**19,426**	**34**	**3,383**	**7,170**	**10,031**	**7,292**	**3,381**	**720**	**51,437**

Source: Offices of the Deputy Commissioners, Districts of Assam, 1947–2004.

of affected people increases to five times, that is, to 2.5 lakh. For a small state like Assam, the number of displaced persons is very large indeed.

Table 3.21 lists the project-wise number of affected persons in Assam. In total, 2,90,083 persons were affected by the process of land acquisition. Of course, this number does not include a large number of people affected by land acquisition by the government and forest department. These affected people, notwithstanding the period of their occupation, are not included as PAPs and hence they are not · entitled to any kind of compensation from the government. This number is an underestimation of the total number of PAPs.

However, Table 3.21 based on government data does not reflect the exact situation—it reflects only a part of it. Perhaps the development projects affected the livelihood of a much larger number of people. For example, Fernandes pointed out that in 1970s only 2,553 families were accounted for and compensated out of 9,000 families displaced by the Dumbur project in Tripura (Fernandes 2005: 34). Here, the government did not officially recognize more

TABLE 3.21
Category-wise Number of PAPs 1947–2000

Category	SC	ST	MOBC	GEN	NA	Total
Water Projects	2,376	12,018	1,458	3,190	67,139	86,181
Industry	6	303	0	814	7,000	8,123
Mines	0	0	0	0	110	110
NYD	0	0	0	77	715	792
Defence	193	22	44	2,767	9,449	12,475
Environment	605	1,117	39	2,657	1,11,056	1,15,474
Transport	28	2,965	539	2,684	42,565	48,781
HRD	28	11	55	1,628	770	2,492
Refugee	0	0	0	53	3,091	3,144
Farms	17	83	0	605	446	1,151
Urban Development	0	0	0	160	270	430
Housing	0	0	0	242	220	462
Social Welfare	6	0	0	655	231	892
Tourism	0	0	0	0	55	55
Health	0	6	28	171	3,790	3,995
Education	110	11	6	248	2,481	2,856
Administration	6	28	0	490	2,063	2,587
Others	0	0	0	0	83	83
Total	**3,375**	**16,564**	**2,169**	**16,441**	**2,51,534**	**2,90,083**

Source: Offices of the Deputy Commissioners, Districts of Assam.

than two-third of the displaced people as IDPs. Many development projects in the region have a similar story. For example, the Brahmaputra Board, an organization under the Government of India, estimated the number of displaced people for the Pagladiya Dam Project at 18,743; however the actual number is about 1,05,000. There has been gross underestimation of IDPs in India. The number of families displaced by development projects is surely much larger than what our official data reflects. Similarly, the development projects have affected the livelihood of a much larger population than what has been officially recorded. Brutality of displacement is not confined to physical ejection/dislocation only, it goes far beyond that; it directly affects the livelihood of the displaced people. This again propels a set of interrelated insecurities, impoverishment risks for the displaced people, as rightly pointed out by Michael Cernea (2000: 3659–78). These risks are landlessness, joblessness, homelessness, marginalization, food insecurity, loss of access to common property and services and social disarticulation. All IDPs experience these impoverishment risks to different degrees. Addressing these risks is crucial for proper resettlement and rehabilitation of the displaced population. Unfortunately, the Indian state neither has a proper humane resettlement and rehabilitation policy nor a framework to address the situation of massive displacement of population.

Earlier we presented a few cases of displacement caused by a few projects by using official data. Table 3.22 shows the number of DPs and PAPs during the period 1947 to 2000 caused by the water resource projects in Assam, based on extrapolated data. Three categories of water resource projects together induced displacement of more than 49,977 persons and affected 3,98,835 persons. If we combine the DPs and PAPs it becomes a mammoth 4,48,812 persons in Assam.

Compared to all-India average, Assam is a lowly irrigated state. Still most of its agriculture is dependent on vagaries of nature. The quantum of irrigated land is also low compared to all-India average. The peasants in Assam continue to depend largely on the monsoon rains. Table 3.23 demonstrates the number of persons displaced by various development projects in Assam. This reflects that a large number of people were displaced during the post-colonial period and there has been no respite from this process. The massive land acquisition has not resulted in industrialization of the state in any significant manner.

TABLE 3.22

Estimates of DPs and PAPs caused by Water Resource Projects 1947–2000

Category	DPs	Per cent	PAPs	Per cent	Tribe	Per cent	Others	Per cent	NA	Per cent	Total
Major	27,236	51.66	25,489	48.34	17,285	32.17	20,150	38.83	15,290	29.00	52,725
Medium	5,707	34.09	11,034	65.91	7,729	46.17	4,911	29.34	4,101	25.0	16,741
Minor	17,034	4.49	3,62,312	95.51	1,32,772	35	2,46,574	65	00	00.0	3,79,346
Total	**49,977**	**11.14**	**3,98,835**	**88.86**	**1,57,786**	**35.16**	**2,71,635**	**60.52**	**19,391**	**4.32**	**4,48,812**

Source: Fernandes and Bharali 2006: 86.

TABLE 3.23

Conservative Estimates of DPs/PAPs by Category (Per cent to Total) 1947–2000

Category	DPs	Per cent	PAPs	Per cent	Total	Category (Per cent)
Water Resources	49,977	11.14	3,98,835	88.86	4,48,812	23.51
Industry	14,220	24.63	43,512	75.37	57,732	3.02
Mines	13,680	33.2	27,520	66.8	41,200	2.16
Non-Hydel Power	1,371	18.53	6,029	81.47	7,400	0.39
Defence and Security	3,337	6.62	47,083	93.38	50,420	2.64
Environment Protection	51,016	19.22	2,14,393	80.78	2,65,409	13.9
Transport and Communication	65,904	43.38	84,858	56.62	1,50,762	7.93
Refugee Resettlement	10,500	3.7	2,73,000	96.3	2,83,500	14.85
Farms and Fisheries	10,671	9.37	1,03,218	90.63	1,13,889	5.96
Education	3,097	3.6	82,840	96.4	85,937	4.5
Health	1,008	4.33	22,284	95.67	23,292	1.22
Administration	64,224	19.89	2,58,679	80.11	3,22,903	16.98
Social Welfare	6,212	24.60	19,041	75.4	25,253	1.32
Human Resource Development	4,288	85.19	745	14.81	5,033	0.26
Urban Development	191	15.39	1,050	84.61	1,241	0.06
Housing, Tourism, etc.	0	0	18,045	100	18,045	0.95
Total	**2,99,696**	**16.08**	**16,01,132**	**83.92**	**19,00,828**	**100**

Source: Fernandes and Bharali 2006: 107.

From 16 categories of land acquisition as shown in Table 3.23, we have found that the projects involved in water resource development induced the largest number of DPs and PAPs at 4,48,812, which constitutes nearly as high as 23 per cent of the total DPs and PAPs in Assam. Land acquisition for administration category led to the generation of second highest number of DPs and PAPs, that is, 17 per cent of the total DPs and PAPs. Significantly, the refugee rehabilitation led to the generation of 2,83,500 DPs and PAPs. This amounts to nearly 15 per cent of the total DPs and PAPs of the state during the post-colonial period. It is unfortunate that to rehabilitate a large group of displaced persons, a large number of people belonging to the host society had to become DPs and PAPs.

Most projects under the environment protection category were aimed at controlling perennial flood in Assam's two valleys. However, the intensity of the floods is increasing every year very significantly with an exception in the year 2006. The hard reality is that it is not only floods but also the flood protection projects that are causing massive displacement of population. Environment protection projects induced 2,65,409 DPs and PAPs. In terms of percentage, it is 14 per cent of the total DPs and PAPs in Assam. Similarly, the infrastructure like transport and communication caused the fifth largest number of DPs and PAPs at 1,50,762 persons, amounting to nearly 8 per cent of the total DPs and PAPs in Assam. Surprisingly, if we look at it in a comparative perspective, the number of DPs and PAPs induced by the industrial projects has not been high, that is, only 57,732, and is only 3 per cent of the total DPs and PAPs of Assam. This also demonstrates the low industrial development in the state. Hence, there was not much scope to provide jobs to the DPs and PAPs from the industrial sector. However, when we look at this conservative estimate, the number of DPs is 2,99,696 and PAPs is 16,01,132. This amounts to a massive 19,00,828 DPs and PAPs together for a small state like Assam during the period 1947 to 2000.

From our field experience, we found that there exists a big gap between the two sets of government data, one recorded in the government gazettes and the other in the records of the district administrations/deputy commissioners. The data of the district administrations demonstrate much larger land acquisition and displacement of population from their land and livelihood. Unfortunately, the district administrations, too, did not keep the land acquisition and displacement data carefully. As a result important data has been lost. Whatever data is available, in most cases, is in shambles. It is of utmost importance to keep the data on land, land acquisition, displacement and land alienation properly in the interest of both the state and the people. It is also high time for the government and the social science community to retrieve the lost data and to update the data so as to create a reliable database. We must point out explicitly that it is not only in Assam or for that matter in the North East, but, by and large, data on land ownership and acquisition throughout India is also in shambles. Hence, it is exceedingly important that fundamental changes are brought about in the way land records are maintained and updated periodically.

We must point out that in post-colonial Assam one cannot look into the causes of internal displacement of population through the prism of development alone. In many situations, one person may experience the same kind of displacement more than once. For example, one may become the victim of environment-induced displacement repeatedly. Again, the same person may experience conflict-induced displacement in his/her new place of residence or livelihood. For example, a person displaced by flood or river bank erosion may cross the boundaries of his/her district or region in search of livelihood, where s/he may become a victim of conflict-induced displacement. This very often happens in Assam and the rest of the North East. And 'displaced', which is supposed to be a temporary/transitory status, becomes a permanent one, with the person waiting and struggling to survive in an all-encompassing situation of fear and uncertainty. Once one becomes a displaced person, it becomes very difficult for him or her to get out of the unending cycle of displacement. It seems the displaced people in Assam in most cases, experience displacement more than once; it is a serialized and multiplied experience. Displacement is a continuous process in North East India in different aspects, forms, situations and space; as an inseparable part of the post-colonial political economy of India. The Indian state and its representatives in the North East have largely failed to address the development needs of the people. The post-colonial process of development has been very brutal to large masses of people. Now, a slow and steady emergence of resistance from the grassroots against such brutality of centralized and regimented development process can be observed in North East India.

Here we need to explicitly point out that the market forces are ascending now as a result of globalization under the neo-liberal dispensation in India in which global capital and its financial institutions like the World Bank, International Monetary Fund (IMF), Asian Development Bank (ADB) and others are involved directly and sometimes tacitly in the emerging political economy of development in India.

North East India being a part of the larger political economy of India cannot escape the consequences of a globalized economy. The neo-liberal paradigm of development is bound to displace a much larger population in North East India. Be it mega dam projects or the four-lane highways, they are bound to displace a large number of people from their home, shelter and livelihood besides causing irreparable damage to the ecology. Consequently, the people living at the margins of the society are likely to be marginalized further as a result of globalization of North East India.

Mega projects have global gainers and local losers. The region may develop in symbolic terms. It may have many mega dams, four-lane highways, shopping malls, amusement parks and fashion shows which are not good enough to hide the reality of poverty, inequality and marginalization of local communities. Many of these communities are deeply entrapped in ethnic violence. Ethnic conflict and violence have increased gradually in the North East along with the gradual process of globalization of the region since the nineties of the last century without any tangible sign of its abnegation.

Massive displacement of population has made a large number of people rootless. Displacement is obviously a disintegrative and disempowering process for the people. What we see today is that a much more ruthless and rapid displacement is looming large for an already marginalized people. If the state fails to realize its ethical responsibility to protect the interest of such people and the people themselves fail to stop the development aggression politically, they are bound to experience the ruthless displacement again and again.

There is no alternative but to bring back the issue of land to the centre of the political agenda for the North East. The land question deserves a deeper understanding and a critical introspection by the Left and democratic political forces. One needs to rethink land as an indispensable resource for the people of Assam and the North East.

4

Development, Dam and Displacement

Resistance from the Threatened

Contrary to popular post-colonial expectation, North East India did not receive much attention in the developmental agenda of the post-colonial Indian state; a manner very similar to the legacy left behind by its colonial predecessors. Obviously, this has been a major irritant in the integration of the North East with the rest of the country. The various ethnic movements that emerged during the post-colonial period were also unsuccessful in articulating the question of development with the aspiration of the people. They failed to offer an alternative developmental paradigm and agenda. The peripheral status of the North East continued for a long period of time despite popular protests and several armed struggles. Whatever development has taken place in the region has been largely lethargic and distorted. This significantly affected the region's potential for autonomous growth. In order to get adequate political and economic attention from the Indian state, the region had to wait till it became highly vulnerable to a bewildering variety of ethnic conflicts and consequent violence with periodic lulls. Consequently, the region experienced the process of militarization. For any conflict zone, it is difficult if not impossible to get out of the trap of underdevelopment even if it gets adequate developmental attention from the state at a later stage. This is what has happened to India's North East. Of late, the region has started receiving significant attention of the Indian state; of course, without any paradigmatic change in the approach to development.

The Government of India has pumped huge funds for the development of the region in recent times. It has made a separate ministry named Development of North East Region (DONER) at the centre to take care of the region's developmental needs. Most central grants for the region have been made non-lapsable unlike other Indian states in addition to other economic incentives. Besides, provisions have been made to ensure that each ministry keeps some specific funds reserved exclusively for the North Eastern states. The Government of India also awards 'peace bonus' in monetary terms to an individual state of the region if it succeeds in maintaining peace in the state. Here, the meaning of peace has been used in an extremely narrow sense, that is, the reasonable absence of violent incidents compared to other states of the region.

As a part of its recent developmental initiatives, the centre is planning to convert North East India into a powerhouse for India by trapping its hydropower potential to the maximum. In order to achieve this ambitious developmental goal, the centre has approved 145 dams (see Sethi 2005: 32 for details) to enhance and ensure India's energy security in future. About a dozen of these dams are already in the pipeline and a few have been completed. Needless to say, the inventory of dams in the pipeline includes many mega dams for the region. We must point out here that besides transforming the landscapes rapidly, intentionally and profoundly, the mega projects inherently induce displacement of population (Gellert and Lynch 2003: 1). Obviously, North East India cannot escape such transformation given the kind of development that is going to take place in the region within the neo-liberal framework.

Here, it would be of crucial importance to look into what Patrick McCully (2003) observed about big dams:

> Big dams are plain bad. They flood people out of their homes and off their lands; wipe out endangered habitats and species; spread water-borne diseases; deprive flood plains of the water and sediments of life-giving floods (while increasing the damage floods cause to people); ruin beautiful landscapes and submerge places of great cultural or spiritual importance. And that's just a partial charge sheet....

He further observes:

> Big dams even cause earthquakes (because of the weight of water
> in reservoirs), release greenhouse gases (because of the rotting of
> flooded vegetation), destroy marine fisheries (because they disrupt
> river-borne flows of freshwater and nutrients into oceans) and
> lead to coastal erosion (because the sediments that eventually fill
> reservoirs would previously have flowed out through estuaries
> and then been washed back by waves to protect the shoreline).
> Occasionally, they collapse and drown people. In the world's
> worst dam disaster—a mega-catastrophe that struck central
> China in 1975 when two large dams burst—as many as 2,30,000
> people died....

What has made the Indian state so generous to the region in recent
times that it is prepared to invest in highly expensive mega dams from
the public exchequer? Significantly, the Indian state has gradually
retreated from its democratic commitment to the people in providing
basic services like education, health, shelter, safe drinking water, electricity and sanitation, etc., in the wake of market-driven globalization
of its economy under the neo-liberal economic discourse. Yet, the
state is prepared to meet such huge financial liability in order to construct dams. Of course, a large chunk of finance is likely to come
from global financial institutions as loans with unavoidable strings
attached to it. What are the reasons for such a developmental adventure at the beginning of 21st century? Though it is very difficult, yet
it would be of crucial importance to seek answers to these questions
in the context of North East India.

One can observe the decline in the rise of mega dam projects globally and in the developing countries, too, including India during
the last part of the 20th century. Anti-dam movements became pro-
minent and powerful during this period and largely succeeded in
building up a global network of resistance movements. The anti-
dam movements have become a very powerful category of New Social
Movements cutting across the national, geographic, class and gender
boundaries. Similarly, the issues of displacement, resettlement and
rehabilitation, equity and justice, utility and efficacy of the mega dams,
impacts of dam on the environment and biodiversity, and the question

of human rights and particularly the rights of the indigenous/tribal people who had to bear the brunt of displacement disproportionately emerged very prominently in public discourse. Proliferation of information and knowledge about the efficacy and the negative impacts of dams alerted civil society organizations (Alvares, C. and Ramesh Billorey 1988, Bavisker 1995, Centre for Science and Environment 1982, International Congress on Dams 1994, McCully 1996, World Bank 1992, World Commission on Dams 2000, Thakkar 2000, Roy, 2001, etc.). The Bhakra Nangal Project, which has been regarded as the propeller of the Green Revolution in Punjab and Haryana, has also been questioned. In his comprehensive study *Unravelling Bhakra: Assessing the Temple of Resurgent India*, Shripad Dharmadhikary has virtually demystified the myth built up for over 40 years (Menon 2005: 4). The state is yet to rehabilitate 7,200 Bhakra displaced families. Dharmadhikary observed that the Bhakra is a classic example of short-term benefits and long-term catastrophe (ibid.). All this severely interrogated the entire gamut of post-colonial development paradigm and wisdom of going in for mega dams; and the dam proponents had no convincing answers to these questions. Defending dams has become increasingly indefensible. Some countries that had built dams enthusiastically, began decommissioning them.

In India too, the emergence of popular and powerful dam resistance movements like *Narmada Bachao Andolan*, *Tehri*, *Silent Valley*, *Subarnarekha*, *Koel Karo* and others raised these questions very pertinently. The Silent Valley project had been abandoned because of pressure from the anti-dam movement backed by an international network. Such pressure also forced global financial institutions like the World Bank to retreat from their commitments in two mega dams including the very highly visible Narmada project. These movements, particularly the *Narmada Bachao Andolan*, were successful in raising their voice at the World Commission on Dams (WCD Report 2000). These movements have been able to draw the attention of the international community and have successfully built up a network at the global and national level. As a new category of social movements, they have been successful in expanding their support base as well as organizational structure while remaining highly visible. They have been able to push forward some highly visible leaders and star campaigners. They have been successful in drawing media coverage nationally and globally. In the process, going in for new mega dam projects have become somewhat difficult in recent times in India. Almost all the mega dam projects under construction got delayed by years together and consequently the cost accelerated immensely. Quite a few fatal accidents during the construction of dams, siltation of reservoirs, dam bursts, panic discharge of water, severe effects on biodiversity, failure to control flood and above all, the failure to generate the stipulated level of electricity together with their incalculable environmental, social, cultural and psychological costs have weakened the justification for mega dams in India in the recent times. Very recently it has been pointed out that large dams in India are responsible for about a fifth of the country's total global warming impacts. The estimates also reveal that Indian dams are the largest global warming contributors compared to all other nations (see Press Release 2007). Consequently, it has become increasingly difficult for the state to go in for mega dam projects in mainland India.

In a recently published book, it has been stated that

technical [such as possible lack of sites], financial and economic factors have clearly made big dam less attractive ... they do not at all tell the whole story. Political-economic dynamics have increasingly contributed to the decreasing financial viability of and changing cost-benefit calculations regarding big dam building (Khagram 2004: 9).

Now, ultimately it is 'politics' that has decisively slowed down the process of growth of mega dams. Khagram further observed that

the unexpected emergence and unexpected strength of transnationally coordinated action—constituted primarily by nongovernmental organizations and social movement—has dramatically altered the dynamics of big dams from the local to the international levels (ibid.: 3).

As India is aspiring to become a global economic power, it must be able to ensure and enhance its energy security. As per official data, by the end of the 20th century, only 55.80 per cent of households in India had electricity connectivity for lighting their homes (Census of India 2001). Still 43.60 per cent of the Indian households use kerosene as an energy source for lighting their homes (ibid.). This reflects very clearly that as high as 44 per cent of the Indian households still do not have electricity. And those who have it, are victims of inadequate service. They very often experience load shedding. Almost all state electricity boards in India have been unable to supply power to all their consumers all the time. India is experiencing a severe deficit in power generation and distribution. Power crisis has become perennial. Very significantly, this found reflection on the eve of the 59th Independence Day address of the President of India, A.P.J. Abdul Kalam, to the Indian nation. Instead of the conventional speech on constitutional, political and economic issues, the President had chosen to talk on an unconventional issue like 'energy security' (for details see Special Correspondent 2005). This unambiguously demonstrates India's present power crisis and future energy insecurity.

The Presidential address also mentioned the imperative of harnessing the hydroelectric potential. Electricity generation needed to be increased to meet the demands of India's growing population and expanding economy. Unfortunately, most state electricity boards despite engaging in a virtual monopoly, proved inefficient both in generating and distributing electricity. They have also failed to stop the power theft. The recent restructuring of the state electricity boards as a part of the Structural Adjustment Programme guided by the World Bank and its associate, the ADB, has not improved the situation either. In many cases, the situation has further worsened. The state policy on the power sector has been disastrous for the country and the people. Most towns and cities throughout India including Delhi, face a regular shortage of power supply. The private sector too has failed to emerge as an alternative power generator and supplier. Some adventures with privatization, like the deal with the US multinational 'Enron', became an embarrassment for the government. India is in dire need to avoid the power crisis and enhance its energy security simultaneously as it enters the 21st century with a dream of becoming a global economic and military power.

It has been increasingly realized in the face of prolonged political disturbances, unending conflicts and violence, that North East India needs much more attention in the development agenda of the Indian state than ever before. Moreover, in the wake of globalization, the capacity of the state to develop a region only through the state initiative has been substantially constricted by international financial institutions. However, the power sector remained largely open for state investment in India. Hence, it has gone in for as many projects as possible for the generation of electricity. We have already mentioned the possible difficulties of the Indian state in going for mega dam projects in mainland India. However, the situation in North East India is somewhat different. Thus the Government of India is planning about 168 dam/hydroelectric projects in North East India. It has been estimated that the North East has the potential to generate 38 per cent of India's total hydroelectric power potential (Fernandes 2004). In order to have mega projects one needs space, in geographical sense, and North East has that space in abundance, particularly in the hill regions. Except the plains of Assam, Manipur and Tripura, the rest of the region is covered by hills and numerous forests and is thinly populated. The density of population of Arunachal Pradesh is the lowest in India. The density of population per square kilometre in Arunachal Pradesh is only 13 persons as against 312 for India and 340 for the neighbouring state of Assam in average (Census of India 2001). In terms of area, Arunachal Pradesh is the largest among the North Eastern states. But its population is less than the actual population of Guwahati. Hence, Arunachal Pradesh has been chosen for as many as 89 (see Sethi 2005: 32) dam projects out of the 168 projects meant for entire North East India including the largest dam project in Asia; the Lower Subansiri Project (henceforth LSP).

Table 4.1 demonstrates the enormous power potential of North East India. Among the North Eastern states, Arunachal Pradesh has the highest potential. According to this estimate, Arunachal Pradesh is capable of generating 26,756 megawatt of electricity, which represents 84 per cent of the total potential of entire North East India. Besides, about 65 per cent of total hydroelectric projects meant for the North East will be located in Arunachal Pradesh alone (ibid.: 32). The availability of vacant space particularly in Arunachal Pradesh is likely

TABLE 4.1
State-wise Hydroelectric Power Potential of North East India in Megawatt

Assam	351	1.10
Arunachal Pradesh	26,756	83.99
Meghalaya	1,070	3.36
Manipur	1,176	3.69
Tripura	9	0.03
Mizoram	1,455	4.57
Nagaland	1,040	3.26
Total	**31,857**	**100.00**

Source: Anon 2004, Presentation to the Union Power Ministry, National Hydroelectric Power Corporation (NHPC), Delhi (quoted from Sethi 2005: 35).

to help minimize displacement of population. Perhaps, this is the biggest advantage for the state. Besides, India's improved diplomatic relationship with China is also a significant factor here in such massive unprecedented allocation of a series of mega dams in Arunachal Pradesh. All these projects have been cleared after the transformation of Indo-Chinese relations. Notwithstanding facilitating the formation of Tibetan government in exile under the leadership of the Dalai Lama almost half a century back, now India no longer raises the Chinese 'occupation' of Tibet or the question of Tibet's independence/autonomy seriously. Similarly, China too now neither questions seriously the integration of Sikkim nor Arunachal Pradesh with India. This tacit mutual understanding under the changed global and regional, political as well as economic compulsions has also drastically changed the attitude of the Indian state from military-strategic concern to developmental concern. This found reflection in the opening up of the Nathula pass for trade between India and China. It must be pointed out that Arunachal Pradesh did not get any significant project for a long time during the post-colonial period. Now, it has been planned to convert Arunachal Pradesh into the powerhouse of India by exploiting its hydropower potential.

It would be important to recollect here that the Central Electricity Authority (CEA) of India, in its Preliminary Ranking Study of potential hydroelectric schemes conducted for all river basins in India gave the highest marks to the Brahmaputra river systems in October 2001. Accordingly, 149 out of 168 schemes in total in this basin got the highest priority, which was supposed to indicate their high viability (Menon, et al., 2003: 133). The study claims to have examined '10 major aspects, which play a vital role in the development of hydro projects'. The 168 schemes considered by the ranking study have a cumulative installed capacity of 63,328 MW and 149 of these were given ranks A and B, indicating high viability. These schemes will be developed by agencies such as the National Hydro-electric Power Corporation (NHPC), North Eastern Electric Power Corporation (NEEPCO), the Brahmaputra Board and State Electricity Boards, and a major portion of this power will be sent to other parts of the country. Apart from these large projects, over 900 mini and micro hydel projects have been identified to meet the local needs of the North East (Menon et al. 2003). Obviously, this is an unprecedented development for the region.

Table 4.2 demonstrates the Preliminary Feasibility Reports (PFRs) under 50,000 MW for hydroelectric generation initiatives in Arunachal Pradesh alone. If these projects are implemented then the state will have to acquire a massive 16,218.44 hectares of land in order to impound water in large storage reservoirs and other related construction for the generation of electricity. These projects are sure to displace a large number of people, disrupt their livelihood and community life very significantly in addition to causing severe damage to fragile ecology and biodiversity.

These projects, according to the proponents, are aimed at making North East the power generator and supplier to the rest of India. However, it seems all these projects have grossly ignored the ecological vulnerability of Arunachal Pradesh and the rest of North East India. Be it Tehri in northern India or Subansiri in the North East, both are an integral part of the fragile Himalayan ecology. Besides, the region is highly vulnerable to earthquakes. It experienced several earthquakes of very high intensity. The 1950 earthquake devastated the lower portion of the river Subansiri, which severely affected the then undivided Lakhimpur district and the famous river island Majuli. Commuting by road in the ecologically fragile hilly areas of the North East is difficult because of the perennial problem of landslides caused by rains on the soft hills. Ironically, while the North East can export its power to the rest of India, it cannot export

TABLE 4.2
Hydroelectric Initiative in Arunachal Pradesh (PFRs under 50,000 MW)

Scheme	River/Basin	Installed Capacity (in megawatt)	Submergence Area (in hectares)
Angoline	Dihang-Dibang	375	94.00
Amulin	Dihang-Dibang	420	69.56
Asshupani	Dihang-Dibang	30	20.50
Attunli	Dihang-Dibang	500	50.75
Badao	Kameng	120	11.20
Bhareli I	Kameng	1,120	715.53
Bhareli II	Kameng	600	357.00
Chanda	Kameng	110	8.33
Demwe	Lohit	3,000	1,525.00
Dengser	Subansiri	552	231.56
Dibbin	Kameng	100	6.40
Doimukh	Subansiri	150	565.00
Elango	Dihang-Dibang	150	54.38
Emini	Dihang-Dibang	500	166.00
Emra II	Dihang-Dibang	390	109.50
Etabu	Dihang-Dibang	165	5.20
Etalin	Dihang-Dibang	4,000	202.00
Hirong	Dihang-Dibang	500	200.00
Hutong	Lohit	3,000	1,519.76
Kalai	Lohit	2,600	1,296.70
Kameng Dam	Kameng	600	3,764.00
Kapaklyak	Kameng	160	544.00
Kurung I and II	Subansiri	330	2,025.00
Mithudon	Dihang-Dibang	400	132.00
Mirak	Dihang-Dibang	141	39.25
Naba	Subansiri	1,000	81.28
Nalo	Subansiri	360	283.80
Naying	Duhang-Dibang	1,000	37.30
Niare	Subansiri	800	48.25
Oju I	Subansiri	700	72.30
Oju II	Subansiri	1,000	27.30
Pakke	Kameng	110	2.08
Papu	Kameng	200	127.00
Phanchgung	Kameng	60	7.80
Rigong	Dihang-Dibang	150	—
Seba	Dihang-Dibang	80	31.00
Simang	Siang	90	139.22
Talong	Kameng	300	1,006.00
Talong Warang	Kameng	30	1.70
Tato II	Dihang-Dibang	700	200.00
Tenga	Kameng	600	260.00
Urung	Kameng	100	3.00
Total		**27,293**	**16,218.44**

Source: *The Hindu Survey of Environment* 2006: 149.

its risks and vulnerabilities associated inseparably with the mega dam projects to the rest of India.

Goswami and Das (2003: 14) have observed:

> In view of the inadequate knowledge base, lack of systematic data over an adequate time span and across diverse terrains and considering the intense dynamism and immense scale of the geophysical process of the Himalayas, *the wisdom behind constructing large dams in the Himalayas raises more questions than can possibly be answered* (emphasis added).

They further added:

> Besides, given the raging controversies over issues such as inappropriate assessment of environmental and social impacts, lack of transparency and public participation in the decision-making process and displacement of local communities and loss of their land and livelihoods, the question assumes further complexity (ibid.).

It seems the state neither posseses adequate knowledge base nor relevant dependable data, which are preconditions for embarking upon such mega projects with a large complex series of risks. Not only that, whatever data the state has, it is reluctant to share the same with the people. That has made the people apprehensive of the intentions of the state and the beneficiaries of such mega projects.

In recent times, the mega dam projects have been facing serious scrutiny from various quarters; civil society organizations, social activists, popular movements, environmentalists, development critics, human rights and humanitarian communities. Disputes have even gone to judiciary for adjudication. Perhaps the judiciary is not yet adequately prepared to adjudicate such new areas of conflict and differences of opinion. However, the efficacy of the large reservoir based hydroelectric projects has been challenged by examining the Indian experience. With the help of data released by the Central Electricity Authority, Thakkar (2004) has shown very pertinently that there exists a large gap between the financial investment in and the generation of hydroelectric power. He has pointed out clearly that despite increasing investment in hydroelectric projects, there has been no matching increase in the power generation, rather the power generation has declined from 82,712 million units in 1994–95 to 73,775 million units in 2003–04. This decline is almost a massive 9,000 million units (Thakkar 2004). This has unmistakably demonstrated that the returns from large hydroelectric projects in India are declining even as investments are increasing over the years (ibid.). This is clearly evident from Figure 4.1.

FIGURE 4.1
India's Hydroelectric Power: Installed Capacity and Generation 2004

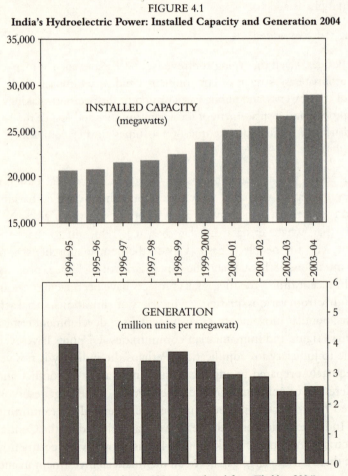

Source: Central Electricity Authority 2004 (reproduced from Thakkar 2004).

At a time when the Government of India should have become cautious and introspective about the hydroelectric projects from its own past experience, it has, on the contrary, embarked into an unprecedented number of hydroelectric projects in North East India, in general, and Arunachal Pradesh, in particular, with a large set of risks and vulnerabilities. Thakkar (2006: 69) observes, 'We can learn a lot from our experience of large dams over the past. Large sections of Indian society and economy would suffer very badly if we do not learn those lessons'. It would be important to recollect here the very often quoted statement of the first Prime Minister of India, Jawaharlal Nehru, in praise of the Bhakra Nangal Dam as the 'modern day temple of India'. However, later on even Nehru changed his assumption about big dams on the basis of his own critical understanding as is evident from the following statement:

> I have been beginning to think that we are suffering from what we may call a disease of gigantism (quoted in McCully 1996: 23).

However, the fascination for gigantism has been continuing unabated in the context of state-sponsored development projects. Obviously, the mega dams are the most visible example of such gigantism in India. For the state, it symbolizes power and modernity.

What has been the response of the state governments towards such developmental adventure of the central government which does not take its own people and ecology at the centre of its planning and implementation? Now, because of financial incentives from such projects and ensured source of power supply of which 12 per cent of the total power generated would be given free to the host state, most North Eastern states have hastily accepted such projects.

It seems the Arunachal Pradesh government too is allured by the revenue potential of the hydroelectric projects. According to Chhackchhuak (2006: 80):

> The State Government calculates that at the rate of around Rs 20,000 per MW—an amount newly negotiated with private developers, J.P. Associates, Reliance Energy Ltd and the D.S. Constructions over and above what the national undertakings are offering—they would be floating in "Hydro dollars just as the Arabs are floating

in Petro dollars," to quote the government's Hydroelectric Power Policy enunciated in August 2005. The government argues that this amount will enable the state to source its own resources and cease being dependent on Central grants, while the dam building process will 'automatically' bring about development such as roads, hospitals, schools and other infrastructure.

Besides, for the hill areas/states in the North East, forest is the major resource. However, because of the Supreme Court's judgement one cannot use the forest for commercial purposes. This has affected the tribal communities and their states severely for several years now. The dams have opened up new possibilities for an alternative means of finance generation for these states at least for sometime. Hence, from the national capital to the state capitals, the dams have become acceptable almost without any conditions and rigorous scrutiny of their socio-economic, environmental, cultural, political and psychological impacts. In the absence of strong resistance movements, it has become easier for the state in embarking into such mutually beneficial ventures based mainly on techno-finance cost benefit analysis. Like all other state-sponsored projects in the past, these projects too are not transparent and have grossly ignored the impact on the environment, people and biodiversity.

Needless to say, North East India is recognized as one of the 25 biodiversity hotspots in the world. This region is also the home of an enormous tribal population. Out of seven North Eastern states, the tribals are a majority in four states. In the remaining three states too, tribal people have a very significant presence. All the mega power projects are to be located mainly in tribal areas. Besides tribal people in the hills, these projects will obviously affect a large number of non-tribal people in the plains of the entire North East. It seems, the state is going in for such ambitious projects without taking the threatened people of the region into confidence.

It would be crucial to understand the response of the people for whom such projects are ostensibly intended. At the governmental level, there has been no dispute on the need for such massive power projects. However, these projects are not transparent. People's right to information has been virtually ignored and not respected. It has not specified the inseparable impacts of dams on society, culture, environment and biodiversity. The displacees of development have virtually remained invisible. They became neither object nor subject of focus for the media. The emerging civil society, too, has not given significant attention to the problem of development-induced displacement. The state, too, remained almost silent and oblivious to the problem of massive displacement of population and the consequent misery it caused to the masses, particularly the tribal people, through its development projects. It has been reported that the massive LSP has not mentioned about 14 villages to be affected by the project (Sethi 2005: 28). Besides, most of the indigenous people of Arunachal Pradesh live in the small valleys surrounded by mountains. These are also their prime agricultural land and source of livelihood. Most of these valleys are likely to be submerged in the big reservoirs meant for impounding water in order to generate electricity. Besides the large reservoirs are likely to shorten both the space and the cycle of the traditional slash and burn, that is, the *Jhum* method of cultivation. Needless to say, in North East most of the hill tribals are used to the traditional *Jhum* cultivation. These reservoirs will directly reduce the quantum of arable land in Arunachal Pradesh besides affecting the livelihood, community structure, economy and ecology, negatively.

The misery of the tribal people remains unarticulated as they are unable to assert their apprehensions and collective voice directly and forcefully. In the North East, almost the entire political space has been occupied by emerging ethnicity and its resultant violence since India's independence. Excessive and obsessive engagement with the bewildering variety of ethnic politics of identity has relegated some major economic and environmental issues faced by the region and the people to the periphery. Ethnic politics failed to articulate the question of massive displacement of population and continuous generation of IDPs of all kinds in North East India. Hence, there was neither any significant resistance from the weaker and smaller communities, nor from the larger society in which they all live. Thus, the state had the monopoly in the decision-making and implementation of the development projects from above. Politicians, bureaucrats, experts and contractors collectively decide the development agenda for the people within the framework prescribed by global capital and their financial institutions. The common people virtually have no rights to decide their development agenda. It comes from above, based on top-down approach. The mainstream development discourse has remained highly centralized and regimented in nature. Right or wrong, it 'must be implemented' as per the centralized agenda, totally ignoring the grassroots reality and the people for whom the development is intended. All this continued to happen till the end of the 20th century. However, one finds a gradual qualitative change in the politics of the region. Internal displacement of population induced by political conflict, environmental degradation and development is emerging slowly as a public and rights issue simultaneously. We can look into the gradual emergence of popular resistance against mega dams and its consequent threat to displacement of population in the name of development from the beginning of the 21st century. Besides displacement, these new movements have raised the question of environmental sustainability of such mega projects. In the process, they are interrogating the entire post-colonial discourse on development and preparing themselves to resist the developmental brutalities on the people and their land.

It is important to scrutinize a few mega dam projects in three North Eastern states—Arunachal Pradesh, Assam and Manipur—in order to understand the response of the 'threatened' people. For this, we have taken up the popular resistance against the Siang and Lower Subansiri Dams in Arunachal Pradesh, Tipaimukh Multipurpose Hydro-electric Project in Manipur and Pagladiya Dam Project in Assam. These case studies are based on extensive field visits. We must note that all these attempts at resistance have not turned into full-blown social movements. But all these movements may be categorized as New Social Movements (NSMs) based on new differences rooted in the opposition to the state-sponsored development process. And most of these NSMs have not completed their career. They are still at the early stage of their career. Hence, what we are studying may remain somewhat tentative, temporal and fluid in the final analysis. Yet, this is likely to help us understand the post-colonial political economy of development on one hand and the process of democratic consolidation at the grassroots level on the other. This would obviously help us in understanding the functional as well as qualitative aspects of the contemporary Indian democracy and the Indian state simultaneously.

Popular Response to Mega Dams

A. Siang, Subansiri and Others

Both the people and the government of Arunachal Pradesh looked very happy and satisfied with the unprecedented decision of the Government of India of granting many development projects in the form of mega dams to generate electricity virtually at one go. We have already explained some of the reasons behind going in for granting such a large number of hydroelectric projects to Arunachal Pradesh. Obviously, it was aimed at converting Arunachal Pradesh into a powerhouse to meet India's energy needs. In the process, it was hoped that these projects would bring immense financial, power and employment benefits to the underdeveloped state and its indigenous people. However, as the projects are being implemented, people have gradually become restless and apprehensive of the negative impacts of such mega projects. Consequently, the state government too has become introspective about the question of dam and development contrary to its initial euphoria.

An MoU was signed in 2000 between the then Chief Minister Mukut Mithi and the NHPC in order to build a series of mega dams. Three such dams are planned to be built; at Pugging in the Upper Siang district, at Ranging in the East Siang district (near district headquarters, Pasighat) and at Payum in the West Siang district. The Upper Siang project alone is aimed at generating massive 11,000 megawatts of electricity. This is going to be the largest hydroelectric project in India. The height of the dam is 257 metres. Following the signing of the MoU, the NHPC started their preliminary work to go ahead with the ambitious series of hydroelectric projects to generate power mainly for consumption outside Arunachal Pradesh and the North East. If the Upper Siang project is commissioned, it will submerge about 200 villages inhabited by indigenous tribal people. Besides adversely affecting the fragile natural environment and rich biodiversity, these series of mega projects will displace an estimated 2,00,000 tribal people and disrupt their community life abruptly and block their access to the natural resources. It has been estimated that if all the projects are implemented, then it will lead to the displacement of 20 per cent of the total population of Arunachal Pradesh.

Accepting the *Narmada Bachao Andolan* (NBA) as their reference group, the people of Siang districts have formed an organization named *Siang Valley Bachao Committee* (SVBC) against commissioning the mega hydroelectric projects in Siang districts. They have been able to gradually build up a popular resistance against the projects. The chairman of the SVBC observed (*The Assam Tribune* 2000):

> ... if the project comes up, it means 52 years of economic development of the area after independence like roads, bridges, culverts, buildings and agricultural fields, forestry and industries including 15 towns and semi-towns will be under water, which will be irreparable loss for the people of Siang.

In addition to a series of Siang dams, the LSP is also facing stiff resistance from the people of Arunachal Pradesh and Assam. The LSP now under construction is located at Gerukamukh, a place at a distance of 471 kilometres from Guwahati. About 90 per cent of the project area falls within the territory of Arunachal Pradesh and the remaining 10 per cent falls under Assam. Perhaps for the first time a mega hydroelectric project is being located in two states simultaneously. It must be pointed out that in order to enter Arunachal Pardesh, any non-Arunachali Indian citizen requires an Inner Line permit.

The LSP is expected to generate 2,000 megawatts of electricity. The height of the dam is expected to be of 116 metres. The total length of the reservoir up to the highest level upstream is expected to be 70 kms. Its water reservoir will submerge 3,436 hectares of land. This includes a large tract of forest land. For example, submergence will include 508 hectares of land of Banderdewa Forest Division, 980 hectares of Hapoli Forest Division, 1,225 hectares of Along Forest Division, 358 hectares of Daparijo Forest Division in Arunachal Pradesh and 365 hectares of Dhemaji Forest Division in Assam. Besides, the LSP is going to submerge 42 hectares of land of the famous

Tale Valley Sanctuary (TVS henceforth). The government declared 337 square kilometre area of the Tale Valley's total 515 square kilometre as the TVS in 1995 in order to protect its rich biodiversity and particularly to protect a few rare species of birds. Very significantly, Birdlife International declared TVS an 'Important Bird Area' (IBA). It would be important to mention here that Arunachal Pradesh is the second crucial biodiversity hotspot in the world. Arunachal Pradesh alone has one-fifth of India's 25,000 varieties of trees and plants (Pegu 2004: 23). Well-known naturalist of North East, Anowaruddin Choudhury observed:

> Notable endangered species that I have recorded in the last decade in the vicinity of the dam site and submergence area are tiger, leopard, clouded leopard, marbled cat, dhole (wild dog), geur, serow, capped langur, slow toris, and gharial, *all listed in schedule I of the Indian Wildlife (Protection) Act 1997* (quoted in ibid.: 23, emphasis added).

The people are worried because the LSP, in their perception, is going to harm the endangered plants and animals simultaneously in a so-called protected area. These protected areas were created in order to provide much needed refuge to the endangered plants and animals in the face of rapidly shrinking natural habitats.

Besides severely affecting the fragile environment, the rich biodiversity, particularly the rare variety of aquatic and wild animals of the region, the LSP has already blocked a natural elephant corridor to pave the way for construction. The Himalayan foothills between Arunachal Pradesh and Assam have been the natural habitats of wild elephants for ages. The LSP's insensitiveness has harmed animals. Anowaruddin Choudhury observes very pertinently:

> The presence of over 15,000 workers at Gerukamukh will seriously hamper elephant movement. From Dulangmukh, the animals cross the Subansiri and move along the southern edge of Gerukamukh housing complex built in 1980 and subsequent road construction has already disturbed the elephant. This forest belt in Assam–Arunachal Pradesh has over 500 elephants and blocking this corridor through further development and disturbances will be disastrous (ibid.: 23).

The NHPC ignored such warnings and consequently, the corridor remained blocked. Because of the gradual reduction of natural habitats for elephants, the man–animal conflict has increased substantially, particularly in North East. The human casualty is also increasing due to the accentuation of the conflict. The people of the area complained that because of the blockade of natural elephant corridor, the elephants very often intrude into human habitation and cause damage to crop, property and human lives.

As per the estimate of 2002, the LSP is likely to cost a staggering Rs 6,608 crore and the project is likely to be completed in 2010. This is going to be the second largest power project in Asia. However, the area in which the project is located has been highly vulnerable to earthquakes. The great earthquakes of 1897 and 1950 which had an intensity of 8.9 on the Richter scale, devastated this area very severely. The memory of the devastation of the 1950 earthquake is very fresh among the older generation of the area.

Significantly, though the project is located mainly in the thinly populated Arunachal Pradesh, it will directly displace and affect the livelihood of about 8,000 people. The NHPC remained silent on this issue. From the very beginning, the LSP, like many other mega projects, has remained non-transparent and hence the people have been in the dark for a long time. With the beginning of the construction of the LSP, the people have raised some very uncomfortable questions about the mega dams and their negative and dangerous potential effects before the state. The state has not been able to respond to these questions convincingly. Despite being citizens of a democratic country with the right to information, the threatened people had no clear information about the details of these projects. The NHPC is supposed to hold an open public hearing as per the Environment Protection Act 1986 and amended in 1997 as a precondition to be fulfilled before starting the construction of the LSP. All recorded public hearings, according to the affected people were farcical and fraudulent. The date of the first public hearing was fixed on 8th September 2001 but it neither mentioned the venue nor informed the public about the mandatory nature of the hearing. Consequently, the potential PAPs neither got a chance to know the details of the project nor could they ventilate their apprehensions about the inherent threat to the people, environment and biodiversity. The concerned people alleged that the public hearing exists only in the official files. Such contempt of transparency angered the people deeply. The NHPC behaved like a supra-state institution which is absolutely unbecoming of a public sector organization. Obviously, the lack of transparency and obduracy on the part of the NHPC has made the situation uncertain, and the people apprehensive and restless.

During my field visit a group of threatened people near Chouldhua expressed their lack of confidence on the NHPC. They told that the NHPC is embarking into a massive project yet they lack necessary 'expertise' and 'honesty' to build even a small concrete bridge. The NHPC constructed a small bridge near Chouldhua over a small stream at a cost of Rs 1.5 crore to establish a communication link with Gerukamukh, the site of the LSP project. Even common people saw an incongruity between the quality of construction and the money spent on the bridge, and complained to high officials of the LSP. The NHPC claimed that the bridge will endure for a hundred years. However, within six months of its construction the concrete bridge collapsed. This small event has big implications for the people living downstream of where the project is being implemented. This enhanced and confirmed their fear. They became highly apprehensive of the expertise and honesty of the NHPC and its select band of contractors. The NHPC, which has been entrusted to execute the project, lacks an image that gives credibility to the organization and confidence in the people. The people are apprehensive of the quality of work being carried out by the NHPC in constructing the dams at the height of 116 metres (LSP), 213 metres (Middle Subansiri Project) and 265 metres (Upper Subansiri Project) above the ground level of the river Subansiri in the plains.

In popular perception, it is an arrogant, corrupt and inefficient organization bent on constructing the LSP and subsequently the Middle Subansiri Project and the Upper Subansiri Project by hook or by crook. In popular parlance, it lacks a moral compass, and hence the people feel that it is capable of inflicting severe human and environmental injustice through the LSP. Without taking the people, particularly the threatened people into confidence, the NHPC commenced the construction work. Besides, the NHPC is claiming that the LSP is constructed in such a way that it can withstand any earthquake upto 10 points on the Richter scale. But the people downstream as well as upstream have refused to accept the claim made by the NHPC. It has also been reported in newspapers that the Lt. General (Retired) Ajai Singh, the Governor of Assam, expressed his apprehension about the potential danger of constructing a big dam in an earthquake-prone zone through a letter in 2004 (Bijoy 2005: 5). Even the governments of the two concerned states, Arunachal Pradesh and Assam, were largely kept in dark on various aspects of the entire Subansiri projects by the NHPC.

The NHPC has antagonized the people by hurting their religious and cultural sensibilities. It has been alleged that the NHPC demolished an old *Naamghar*, a place of community worship, as well as cultural activities of the Vaisnavite Hindus on 7th April 2005. The NHPC also destroyed an ancient place of traditional elephant worship without obtaining the consent of the people of Geruka Nalah near Gerukamukh, the site of the project. Both these arbitrary actions have further damaged the 'image' of the NHPC. The People's Movement for Subansiri Valley (PMSV) condemned the action of the NHPC. The people felt that the NHPC has no respect for indigenous people, their religion and culture. The PMSV alleged that despite objections from the local people, the NHPC did not stop their 'sacrilegious acts'. It further claimed that these places of worship had been playing a significant role in the religious as well as cultural lives of the local people. Besides, the unique traditional elephant worship had been drawing a large number of elephants and people to the area (for details, see the Staff Reporter 2005: 3).

The people alleged that from the very beginning the LSP has been very vulnerable to accidents. In an accident on 7th August 2005, lives of 14 labourers were saved miraculously. Massive soil erosion caused by rain blocked a tunnel under construction which trapped 14 labourers who were working there. They remained trapped inside the dark tunnel for nearly 20 hours. The people in the area have alleged that the ordinary labourers have been working at a great risk to their lives at the project site and the NHPC has not adopted adequate safety measures unlike other similar organizations.

The NHPC has been facing serious charges for inappropriate allotment of contracts from smaller to bigger contractors like some transnational corporations. The local people feel that they have been deprived from getting even small contracts which they are quite capable of handling. Even for small works the NHPC is engaging contractors from outside. The way in which a contract worth Rs 1,600 crore was allotted to Alstom of France bypassing the claim of the Bharat Heavy Electricals Limited (BHEL), a Government of India undertaking, provoked the Left MPs to raise the issue in the Parliament and to write a strong letter to the Prime Minister of India. The Indian media, too, covered this widely (for details, see Barooah 2005 and Ramachandran 2005). Besides the Left MPs, very significantly G.E. Vahanvati, the Solicitor General of India expressed his resentment against the improper procedure through which the contract was awarded to Alstom France by depriving BHEL (ibid.). On the other hand, Sontosh Mohan Dev, an MP from Assam and Union Minister of State for Heavy Industries, who is in charge of BHEL, sought the 'kind intervention' of the Union Minister of Power. He also mentioned some serious irregularities in the process of allotting the contracts. He observed that "the French Company has no experience or infrastructure to manufacture the required equipments and should have got disqualified on just that count" (Ramachandran 2005: 34).

It needs to be pointed out explicitly that the NEEPCO, another public sector undertaking under the Ministry of Power, Government of India, which was executing the 60 MW Turial Hydroelectric Project in Meghalaya decided to blacklist the Alstom in early 2005 for its failure to execute the contract for which the Letter of Intent was issued. However, its sister organization, the NHPC, found it suitable for a 2,000 MW power project! People are sceptical about the integrity and competence of the personnel of the organization entrusted to build a mega project in an ecologically fragile region. People are gradually becoming conscious of the negative consequences and threat of big dams, and professional competence and honesty of the builders of such dams. All this has propelled the people both downstream of the project in Assam and upstream in Arunachal Pradesh to fight against the construction of the LSP. The newly emerged Arunachali elites have also realized the risks involved in the mega dam projects. The common people who are being threatened by the LSP are not only contesting the wisdom of going in for such mega dams; they are interrogating the entire gamut of post-colonial development discourse and its implications for the people and the ecology of the North East.

Besides the resistance of the people both in Arunachal and Assam, very significantly the Governor of Assam, the constitutional head of the state, raised objections to and expressed his apprehensions about the LSP. Perhaps this has happened for the first time in India. Nowhere in India, a Governor of a state has ever raised such objections on a mega project sponsored by the state itself.

In an unprecedented development, the state government of Arunachal Pradesh opposed in black and white the construction of mega hydroelectric projects in the state sponsored by the Government of India being executed through the NHPC, NEEPCO, etc. (see A Staff Reporter 2005: 1 and Rina 2005: 13). In a meeting of the National Development Council held in New Delhi on 27 and 28th May 2005, Gagong Apang, the Chief Minister of the state, informed the collective decision of the cabinet that his government had decided not to undertake or allow any new reservoir-based mega dams in Arunachal Pradesh. This is a historically significant development wherein a state government has opposed a development project granted and fully financed by the centre. No state in India ever opposed such centrally-sponsored projects. It would be important to point out here that the governments of Gujarat and Uttar Pradesh/ Uttarakhand always supported the stand of the central government in Sardar Sarovar and Tehri projects, respectively. Both these are centrally-sponsored projects. Despite organized popular opposition to these projects, the state governments always stood by the central government.

But the Arunachal case is unique, wherein the state government decided to respect the voice of the people. For all practical purposes, it endorsed the voice of the people and accepted it as a popular mandate. And consequently, it openly contested the policy and decision of the all-powerful central authority located in New Delhi. This event has a significant potential in redefining the centre-state relations in the context of development. In the history of mega dams in India, this is an unprecedented event.

The arguments put forward by the state government are very similar to the arguments of the opponents of mega dams. The Arunachal Pradesh government asserted that the big storage reservoir had severe negative effects like inundating upstream areas including a large tract of reserved forest, rare flora species, displacement of tribal population from their historical homeland and displacement of animals from their habitat. The government also pointed out that Arunachal Pradesh falls in the highly vulnerable seismic zone-V; the geological structure of the state is highly fragile, and the rich flora and fauna needs to be protected and the topography of the region ideally suits the run-off-the river projects among others. The state government is not opposed to development projects, as long as they are sustainable. As a viable alternative to storage/reservoir dams, it pleaded for qualitatively different and relatively eco-friendly run-off-the river hydel projects. The mega projects should be replaced by risk free micro projects. This case provides a unique opportunity for the centre to rethink its development policy and its implications for smaller states and smaller communities in Arunachal Pradesh and the North East.

Though the state government decided not to undertake or allow any new mega dam projects, it seems the decision of the centre remained intact. Construction of all the mega dam projects already undertaken has been going on unabated despite protest from the state government and the people. However, the centre decided to put on hold other projects in the pipeline. The state government has even approached the Supreme Court to put various projects on hold. These include those proposed by both state-owned power majors, NHPC and NTPC. Without disclosing details, the Union Power Minister very recently said that issues holding up several hydropower projects in Arunachal Pradesh have been resolved paving the way for an MoU for setting up a 21,000 MW generation capacity (*TOI News*, 15th September 2006). It seems that the Government of India is determined to go ahead with its centralized agenda of making Arunachal Pradesh its power-house based on mega hydroelectric projects to overcome India's power insecurity. Power relations between the centre and the state government in power sector, like other sectors of political economy, remains asymmetrical within India's 'federal' polity. In a total turnaround of events, the Government of Arunachal Pradesh signed an MoU on 21st September 2006 with the NHPC, NEEPCO and a joint venture between the state government and the NHPC to commission nine mega hydroelectric projects in order to produce 15,000 MW of electricity in the state at a massive cost of Rs 1 lakh crore. Out of this, Rs 75,000 crore were meant for generation and Rs 25,000 crore for evacuation of power (see Our Bureau 2006B). As per the stipulations of the MoU, while Arunachal Pradesh would be entitled to 12 per cent free power from each of these projects located in the state, additionally, an amount of 1 paise per unit of electricity generated would be contributed by each project to Local Area Development Trust. The money in the Trust would be used to take up developmental activities for people of the affected area (ibid.). Now a tough competition has started between the public sector undertakings and the private corporate houses to take up mega hydroelectric projects in Arunachal Pradesh. Gagong Apang, the Chief Minister at the time of signing of MoUs said aptly:

> Private developers are giving us up to 19 per cent free power from the hydro projects as against 12 per cent given by Central utilities such as NHPC (ibid.).

From the cost involved in just nine mega projects, one can imagine the financial cost likely to be involved in the remaining 150 plus hydroelectric projects being planned in North East India. It seems that the state government was under severe pressure from the central government to accept all the projects though at one stage their voice was quite similar to that of those who are opposed to going in for such mega projects in ecologically fragile Arunachal Pradesh. Even the state government went to the Supreme Court seeking justice in the face of commissioning of mega dam projects. The centre has very successfully co-opted the Arunachal Pradesh government to accept its centralized development paradigm. It seems that the centre is not yet prepared to accept the voice of the smaller states. Even if the smaller state voices its concern, it cannot expect the centre to respect the same. This has amply been proved in the case of Arunachal Pradesh.

While attending the MoU signing ceremony, the Union Power Minister in his speech at Itanagar on 21st September 2006 said emphatically, 'The state government plays a vital role in the development of these projects. It is not only instrumental in the allocations of the projects, *it needs to be involved in the land acquisition and environmental and forest clearance besides law and order and facilitations for timely completion of the projects*' (emphasis added, ibid.). The concerned state government plays a crucial role particularly in land acquisition and in providing environmental and forest clearance for commissioning any centrally-sponsored developmental project in the state. The states, particularly the smaller ones without any significant financial resources, have virtually no option than to toe the line of the centre keeping in view the structure of cosmetic federalism in India. The dams have strengthened the centre's capacity but have reduced the potential of the state. In the process, the dams have become the symbol of power of the Indian state in North East.

Once the Arunachal Pradesh government's position converged with popular voice of the dissenting people, it significantly affected the momentum of the resistance movement against the mega projects. This is because the state government itself took up the cause for which these movements were fighting for. It gave the cause a double legitimacy, that is, from the state government as well as from the people. The state government's turnaround at a later stage rudely shocked the people who expected the state government to take up their cause to the logical end.

However, the anti-dam movement continues despite aberrations caused by the state government. The situation is very similar to the NBA in the aftermath of the Supreme Court judgement in 2000. Because of the NBA's opposition, the World Bank withdrew from financing the Sardar Sarovar Project and the Supreme Court withheld the construction for six long years. All this was a big success for the NBA. The movement consequently expected a favourable judgement. But this was not to be. The Supreme Court's judgement ultimately went in favour of the dam. Of course, one of the three-judge bench dissented the judgement. Ultimately, the judgement of the two judges prevailed (see Jain 2001, NBA 2000). This had shocked the NBA and its supporters throughout the world. But this did not deter the NBA from its long-drawn struggle. Similarly, despite the turnaround of the Arunachal Pradesh government, the anti-dam movement continues in the state and in the downstream areas outside the state. The anti-dam movement not only raised the question of resettlement and rehabilitation of project displaced people, but also of sustainable development, protection of environment and biodiversity, democracy and federalism in India. Perhaps, most importantly, it is challenging the development paradigm of the post-colonial Indian state and searching a new alternative paradigm.

B. Tipaimukh Multi-purpose Project

The Tipaimukh Multi-purpose Project (henceforth TMP), one of the major and ambitious power projects in the North East to be located in the state of Manipur, is in the pipeline for half a century, that is, since 1955. The project site is located at the tri-junction of Assam, Manipur and Mizoram. The government wants to build the 1,500 megawatt TMP at an estimated cost of Rs 2,899 crore at July 1995 price level. By now the estimated cost has gone up four times the original stipulation. It has been estimated that the laying of the grid for TMP will cost an additional Rs 600 crore (Sethi 2005: 35). The proposed TMP—162.8 metre high rock-filled dam—aims basically at preventing the occurrence of flood in the adjoining Barak Valley in southern Assam. This is likely to permanently submerge 275.50 square kilometres of land surface while the water reservoir gets built to impound 15.5 million cubic feet of water. It seems that in size the TMP reservoir will be 75 per cent larger than the Bhakra reservoir. The TMP will submerge 16 villages fully and severely affect another 51 villages. Besides, the proposed dam will submerge altogether 60 kilometres of the existing National Highway 53.

Table 4.3 demonstrates the anticipated loss of property from the TMP. These figures were based on official data available in 1999. The actual loss is likely to be more than what has been described. The data obviously points to the anticipated loss of property which is massive. This loss will directly affect the tribal people living in the proposed project area. This is not only a loss of land but also of livelihood

TABLE 4.3
Anticipated Loss of Property from the TMP in Manipur and Mizoram

		Manipur		Mizoram	
Type of Land	*Rate of Compensation*	*Area in Hectare*	*Amount in Rupees*	*Area in Hectare*	*Amount in Rupees*
Forest	4,375	11,332	4,95,77,500	954	41,73,750
Uncultivated land	5,240	10,979	5,76,39,750	1,220	64,05,000
Private land	8,750	3,010	2,63,37,500	159	13,91,250
Cultivable land	8,750	2,595	2,27,06,250	108	9,45,000
Garden areas	8,750	720	63,00,000	27	2,36,250
Crop compensation	2,835	648.75	18,39,206	27	78,545
Compensation for fruit trees	Approx.		3,87,14,000	Approx.	7,90,000
Government/semi- Government buildings	875	566	4,95,250		2,66,000
Private buildings	437.50	1,006	4,40,125		
Temples/church	17,500	4	70,000	1	17,500

Source: Sinha 1999: 14.

and fragmentation of tribal community life. The project is likely to consume a huge tract of land in a deep interior area. The tribal people are totally dependent on the land and the forest. Most of them are engaged in *Jhumming*—the slash and burn cultivation under a very difficult situation. Besides, this area is rich in horticultural products. Cultivation of paddy, ginger and fruits like orange and guava constitute the major source of income and survival for the tribal people living in the proposed project area. Though the majority of the victims are the tribal people from Manipur, the project also affects a significant number of people from the neighbouring state of Mizoram. Most of the victims are subsistence farmers. The TMP has become a big threat for their subsistence, livelihood and culture.

Besides the submergence of a large tract of forest and agricultural land, the implementation of the TMP will lead to the displacement of over 15,000 people. The displaced tribal people are likely to experience all the impoverishment risks as stated earlier (by Cernea). Here, like in many other similar projects in the North East, the tribal people will be the major victims; the Zeliangrong Nagas and the Hmars will be the direct victims of the project. These two tribal groups are vehemently opposed to the construction of the TMP. The tribal people, under the banner of Committee Against Tipaimukh Dam popularly known as CATD, have started popular resistance movement against the proposed dam. The struggle against this dam began since early 1990s and has seen almost all the major movement groups, NGOs and professionals joining the protest. Some of the major groups that have been part of the collective struggle against the TMP include Hmar Students' Association (HSA), Zeliangrong Union (ZU), Naga Mothers Union, Manipur (NMUM), All Manipur United Club Organization (AMUCO), Naga People's Movement for Human Rights (NPMHR), Citizens' Concern for Dams and Development (CCDD), Action Committee Against Tipaimukh Project (ACATP), United Naga Council (UNC), All Naga Students' Association, Manipur (ANSAM), Naga People Organization (NPO), etc. Cutting across the ethnic divide, the people are fighting against the project. For all these years, these groups have been protesting against the TMP. They have been demanding the central as well as state government and the NEEPCO to abandon the dam.

Ms Aram Pamie, the Secretary of the Naga Women Association of Manipur observed very succinctly in a letter to the editor (*Economic and Political Weekly* 2001: 1054 and 1145):

> The Zeilangrong people who live in these areas, like any other tribal people, do not lead an individualized commodity governed life but live in a well-knit web of community life. Their ancestral emotional bonds to their land—the mother earth, constitute their cultural and psychological frame of mind that cannot be compromised or negotiated. The submergence of the Ahu (Barak) waterfalls, the biggest and most beautiful natural gift in Manipur, will destroy an important aspect of their heritage—the innumerable myths and legends which are an inalienable part of their bank of memories inherited through centuries. The high watermark of the dam will also destroy the five most important lakes located just above the Ahu waterfall where the magical sword of Jadonang, the national hero of Nagas, is believed to be hidden. All these priceless and inalienable part of their cultural heritage cannot be left to the mindless destruction by dam project authorities.

After facing a stiff opposition in Manipur, the TMP is also facing similar opposition in the neighbouring state of Mizoram. It has been reported that the public hearing conducted by the Mizoram Pollution Control Board (MPCB) on 2nd December 2004 at Darlawn witnessed apprehensions that it would affect the indigenous people of the region (Thakuria 2004: 19). The Mizoram-based human rights organizations vehemently opposed the project with the argument that the exercise would adversely affect the local people. They termed this kind of development a contravention to the Constitution where the tribal and their lands are protected (ibid.). However, the smaller voices, smaller identities do not seem to get the attention they deserve from the Indian state. The divide created by the insensitiveness of the state and the sensitiveness of the smaller communities is a complex one. The existing development paradigm is not capable of addressing this tussle.

In his study on socio-anthropological aspects of the TMP, A.C. Sinha observed rightly:

> The Tipaimukh Hydroelectric Project presents contradiction at various levels, between the needs of the plains and the hills, between the perception of the state administration and micro-level tribesmen, between the demand of 'developed' and urbanized plainsmen and the relatively isolated small communities, and between proponents of development and exploitation and the survival and preservation (Sinha 1999: 30). This observation is largely applicable to all other mega dam projects in the North East to a higher and lesser degree.

It would be important to recollect here that the Manipur State Legislative Assembly unanimously opposed the construction of the dam twice, once in 1995 and again as late as in 1998. The Assembly, the highest political decision-making institution at the state level, expressed its deep apprehension about the seismology and environmental aspects of the TMP. However, very surprisingly, Mr O. Ibobi Singh, the present Chief Minister of Manipur, disclosed that his government would go ahead with the TMP. He sees it as a developmental measure and has appealed to the people not to put any hurdle in the construction of the TMP. The Government of Manipur signed an MoU with the NEEPCO in January 2003. Here, one can see the turnaround of the Manipur government on the TMP. On earlier occasions, the Manipur Legislative Assembly emphatically rejected it twice. The opinion on the TMP is also sharply divided; a large number of the non-tribal people in the plains of Manipur support the project while the tribal people in the hills are opposed to the project. The Manipur government since it changed its position, has been trying to convince the opponents of the TMP to support the project in the larger interest of the state. The opponents, however, are not convinced.

It seems the government is determined to go ahead with the TMP despite resistance from the tribal people who are going to be affected severely. It is of course going to be difficult for the government to go ahead with the project in the wake of opposition from the 'indigenous people' of the land. Sontosh Mohan Dev, the Union Minster of State for Heavy Industries who represents the parliamentary constituency of Silchar in the downstream area of the project which is one of the targeted beneficiaries of the TMP, declared that the TMP which has been hanging in the balance for last 50 years is expected to see the light of the day as the major hurdles in implementing the TMP have been gradually removed (*The Assam Tribune*, 22nd February 2005). Neither the concerned minister nor *The Assam Tribune* specified the 'major hurdles'. As the people entrusted to construct the project in an interior area do not feel 'safe', *four battalions of Central Reserve Police Force (CRPF) will be deployed at Tipaimukh and Rs 280.59 crore would be spent for this purpose and the Home Ministry has agreed to bear the expenditure* (ibid., emphasis added).

Not only the Tipaimukh project, other hydroelectric projects are also facing resistance from the potential oustees. For example, the people of the Churachandpur district of Manipur, have been offering resistance to the building of the Khuga dam for a long time. In a police firing on 19th December 2005, three persons were killed while resisting their displacement and construction of the dam on their land. This project started in 1984 is yet to be completed after 22 long years in 2006 (for details see *India Together*: 19th September 2006).

Dispute over construction of mega dams goes far beyond the territory of the nation-state. It has a regional/South Asian dimension too. For example, Pakistan is complaining against India's Baglihar project (for details see Mohanty and Khan 2005: 3155–58). Not only are the potential IDPs and the two tribal communities opposing the construction of the TMP, but also neighbouring Bangladesh is opposed to this project. The Government of Bangladesh has made a request to the Government of India through diplomatic channel not to construct any reservoir/dam in the upstream of the common river. It says that any such construction could dry up two of its rivers, the Surma and Kushiara that pass through the tea growing regions of Bangladesh (*The Assam Tribune*, 14th March 2005: 1). Most of the rivers of the North East flow into the Bay of Bengal after criss-crossing through Bangladesh. Bangladesh is apprehensive of the potential negative impact of such mega projects on their downstream areas. The impact of the TMP goes far beyond the borders of India. Any drastic change in the natural flow of the rivers common to India and Bangladesh has all the potential of creating spillover problems that would go beyond the borders of one country, the way the construction of Kaptai Dam under the East Pakistani military regime had severe spillover problems for India and the North East. It had to accept a large number of Kaptai PAPs belonging simultaneously to ethnic as well as religious minority groups like the Chakmas and Hajongs. They had to cross over to India once the construction of the dam started. A large number of them are still surviving as 'stateless people' in India and waiting indefinitely for elusive Indian citizenship. The TMP has complex internal as well as external implications. Even in the face of prolonged and sustained popular opposition, the Government of India with the support of the Manipur government has decided to go ahead with the commissioning of the TMP. The Prime Minister, supposed to lay the foundation stone for beginning the construction at the stipulated site on 25th November 2006, too experienced opposition. The opponents of the project submitted memorandums and started signature campaigns to scrape the project for good. It would be crucial to understand that all the necessary arrangements were made to invite and receive the Prime Minister of India. The holding of public hearing which is an essential precondition to be met before starting any construction work was decided, at the eleventh hour, to be held on 17th November 2006, at Churachandpur and Tamanglong. The fact that it was organized in a rush, just few days before the foundation laying ceremony, made the people to call it an act of fraudulence.

The Prime Minster ultimately cancelled his programme at the eleventh hour. However, at a later stage, the Union Power Minister laid the foundation stone to formally mark the beginning of the construction. This finally ended all the uncertainties about the project. It seems the centre is determined to commission the TMP, come what may. However, the movement against the dam continues; cutting across the ethnic divide.

C. Pagladiya Dam Project

The Pagladiya Dam Project (henceforth PDP) on the river Pagladiya has been in the pipeline for a reasonably long time. The Pagladiya river is an important tributary of the Brahmaputra and originates in Bhutan. The river flows from Bhutan downwards to Assam plains in the northern bank of the river Brahmaputra. In local folk culture these two rivers are regarded as 'male' rivers. The PDP was originally conceived as a minor flood detention project at an estimated cost of Rs 12.60 crore based on a report of the Central Water Commission way back in 1968–71. It was duly approved by the Planning Commission of India as a flood control project for Rs 12.80 crore at the 1971–72 price level. Later, it was conceived as a power generating project which would also irrigate a large area. The Government of India kept it in cold storage for a long time and revived it only in 1995. The Technical Advisory Committee of the Ministry of Water Resources, Government of India, cleared the project in August 1995. Again the project went into oblivion. However, the Government of India under the National Democratic Alliance (NDA) regime cleared the long pending PDP on 29th November 2000 at a cost of Rs 542.90 crore. Four years later, it was estimated that the cost of the project had reached Rs 1,136 crore (*The Assam Tribune*: 2004: 1).

Ms Bijoya Chakroborty, the Union Minister of State for Water Resources, the lone representative from Assam in the Vajpayee Cabinet, described the project as the 'Gift of Vajpayee' to the people of Assam. As per the definition of the World Commission on Dams (2000), this is going to be a big dam in the technical sense.

The Brahmaputra Board was entrusted with the implementation of the project. As per the plan stipulation, the project is scheduled for completion in 2007. As per plan, a 23 kilometre long and 26 metre (roughly 80 feet) high dam, in order to retain 446 million cubic metre of water in an artificial lake/reservoir, is to be constructed on the upstream of the river Pagladiya in Lower Assam's Nalbari district at Thalkuchi, a site near the Indo-Bhutan international border. The main canal would be 66.2 kilometres long, along with another branch canal of 39.5 kilometres, the total length being 105.7 kilometres. As per official information, the PDP will protect 40,000 hectares of land from flood, irrigate 54,125 hectares of land, and generate 3 megawatt of electricity.

The social cost of the project is incalculable. The proposed reservoir will submerge 38 settled villages, affecting about 12,000 families directly. However, according to Gita Bharali, the PDP will displace 20,000 families (Bharali 2004: 77). The construction of dam, roads, reservoir and canals will lead to the displacement of about 1,05,000 people from their land and homes (Dutta 2003). About 34,000 acres of land will be acquired for the project. Land in the proposed project area is highly fertile. This will directly affect their livelihood. Again, we must point out that most of the potential victims are poor peasants and a large number of them are tribal, mostly Bodos. Besides, the project will totally submerge four high schools, 13 middle schools and 40 primary schools, several primary health care centres, temples, *Naamghars* and other places of worship. It must be pointed out that all the high schools were established by the people initially and later on received grants from the state. All these are very important social assets for the people, which they cannot afford to lose at any cost, like their homes and land.

The government is now proposing to grant Rs 20,800 per displaced family, Rs 1,000 as material grant; and planning to shift the project displacees to a government reserved forest in the same district. However, the site at which the government is planning to shift the displacees is no longer a vacant place; it is already an 'illegally' settled area. The potential victims told us that the place has already been occupied by the East Pakistan refugees and other displaced people of the same district. Nalbari, despite being an overwhelmingly rural

district, is one of the densely populated areas. The district has virtually no land to resettle such large number of displaced peasants. Other
districts are unwilling to accommodate such a vast number of IDPs.
The people are convinced that the government is not in a position
to resettle such a large number of displaced people in the absence
of vacant land in the plains. Now the only option left to the government is to resettle and rehabilitate them in different places.
However, this will lead to fragmentation of the community.
Hence, the people are against rehabilitating the displaced in different places. They feel that such a move would lead to fragmentation of community life which is very dear to them. The leaders of
the movement have a fairly good idea not only about the quantum
but also about the quality of land to which the government proposes
to relocate the displaced. Obviously, the displaced peasants would
not only need land for reconstructing their houses but also agricultural land and water to ensure their survival and livelihood. They
firmly believe that the government has neither adequate land nor
financial resources to provide them a reasonable rehabilitation
package which at least ensures their present socio-economic status
and dignity. An all-encompassing fear of being displaced has severely
affected the people.

Most of the potential displacees are vehemently opposed to the
implementation of the PDP because to them it directly attacks their
right to land and livelihood. Significantly, this area is not flood-prone
unlike the rest of the southern part of the same district, its land is
fertile, and the density of population is low compared to the rest of
the district. To them the project is flawed, non-transparent and
rehabilitation would be an impossible task for the state. Hence, they
are opposed to the project and its consequent massive displacement of population now living in the proposed project area. Some
of them are very deeply scared because they do not have proper
ownership documents for the land on which they were living on
and cultivating continuously for decades together under very difficult
environmental conditions. They fear that like in many other state-
sponsored projects, only those people who have proper land
documents will be resettled and rehabilitated by the government
and the others who have no legally valid documents will be left out

from the purview of the rehabilitation measures. The state obviously looks very mechanically at the legal documents not at the humans/citizens. By such legalistic insensitivity to its own citizens, the state alienates the people who need its protection desperately. Hence, the fear of being displaced looms large over the potential displacees of the PDP, and they have collectively refused and successfully resisted the 'Gift of Vajpayee' since the year 2000. It seems the people are determined to oppose tooth and nail the implementation of the PDP. They are convinced that the project goes against their interest and have successfully built up a collective popular resistance movement against the project.

The Brahmaputra Board prepared a Resettlement and Rehabilitation (henceforth R&R) package at the cost of Rs 47.89 crore. The number of potential project displacees estimated by the Board is 18,743 persons and the R&R package aims at covering them. This is a gross underestimation of the number of potential PDP displacees. Some affected people of the same area will be entitled to the R&R package while some will be left out from it. Therefore, the potential displacees irrespective of entitlement and non-entitlement have rejected this R&R package totally. The people who see themselves as potential victims of the PDP have questioned the democratic commitment and also the credential of the state in the face of a common threat. They further opine that the main emphasis of democracy should be on the security of the lives and livelihood of the citizens—what they call '*Jivan Aru Jivikar Nirapatta*'.

People of the threatened area protested against the proposal of construction of the dam from the very beginning. A people's resistance committee known as 'Pagladiya Bandh Committee' under the chairmanship of Mukundaram Medhi was formed way back in 1968–69 at the time of first investigation for the PDP. Initially PDP was conceived as a minor flood detention project. Even at that time when such projects were worshipped and the dams were regarded as the 'temples of modern India', these people in the remote villages, most of them illiterates, recognized the hidden negative effects of such projects and started their protest against the all-powerful state and the imposition of its development discourse. The voice of these voiceless people succeeded in pushing the proposal in the cold-storage of the state for a reasonably long period of time. However, later on, in 1987 the state government under the leadership of the *Asom Gana Parishad* (henceforth AGP) pressurized the Government of India to revive the PDP as a permanent solution to the perennial problem of flood in the Nalbari district. The people living in the flood plains downstream of the river Pagladiya supported the move of the state government while the people living in the plains upstream of the river in the same district vehemently opposed it. The opinion on the PDP remained divided sharply within the district on the perception of 'winners' and 'losers' from the project. Obviously, the opposition came from the potential displacees of the PDP. In sharp contrast to the supporters of the PDP, the opponents have organized themselves solidly and mobilized support for their cause. And they have shown it through political mobilization and action at the grassroots level.

The resistance against the PDP began alongside the initial stage of investigation for the project in 1968. The very proposal of the PDP made the people restless as they started to look at themselves as the potential victims of the project in the pipeline. Once the AGP started the initiative to revive the project in 1987, the simmering restlessness of the people gradually transformed into a popular resistance movement outside the purview of conventional political parties. The potential displacees convened a general public meeting in 1987 and gave an organizational shape to their resistance movement. They formed an organization named '*Pagladiya Bandh Prokalpar Khatigrasta Alekar Sangram Samitee*' (henceforth Samitee). Since then the collective leadership of the Samitee has been successfully leading the movement. This Samitee has successfully mobilized massive support from the people of the area that was supposed to be submerged under the proposed water reservoir of the PDP. Various social and student organizations, particularly the tribal ones of the area, supported the resistance movement. One of the most significant organizations that supported the movement was the All Bodo Students' Union (ABSU). The ABSU started the Bodo movement soon after the demise of the Assam movement in 1985. Since then, the ABSU remained a very powerful students' organization representing the ethnic voice of the Bodos. ABSU's support gave the movement an additional advantage and clear edge.

With the passage of time, the popular resistance against the PDP is gaining momentum. It has been successful in mobilizing the support of the entire people being threatened by project induced displacement. We must point out that the people supporting the movement belong to various communities sharing a common living space harmoniously over a long period of time. Their unity has been further strengthened by an all-encompassing common threat of being displaced from their home and land. The people living in the proposed project area include Hindus, Muslims and Christians. Community wise, the Asamiyas and Bengalis of different castes, Nepalis, Santhals, Rabhas are living side by side. However, demographically, community wise, the Bodos are the largest group in this area. In other words, the community in this area is multiracial, multireligious, multilingual, multi-ethnic and multicultural in its composition. And, the people here have been living harmoniously despite some aberrations in the wake of the Assam and Bodo movements. Most of these people are peasants and they reflect the fundamental characteristics of a peasant society. Hence, for them land is the only resource that sustains their lives and livelihood. Emotionally too, they are very deeply attached to their land. Unlike any modern society, the sense of community is very strong and cuts across the class and ethnic divide. Resistance against the PDP has further strengthened the inter as well as intra community relations. It would be important to state here that most ethnic/tribal movements in the North East have been by and large, exclusivist in nature. However, this anti-dam movement (though the major component of it are the Bodo tribal) has remained highly inclusivist in nature wherein the tribal and the non-tribal are fighting shoulder to shoulder for a common cause against an all-encompassing common threat. The inclusivist and multi-ethnic character of the popular resistance has been reflected in two recent publications (Deka 2002 and Deka 2004). These two were, in fact, souvenirs of the 17th and 18th biannual conferences of the *Samitee*.

Each souvenir was published in English, Assamese and Bodo in common binding. These two souvenirs reflected the reasons, anger and aspirations of the threatened people of the PDP. Collective efforts of all the ethnic groups living in the area invigorated the movement at the grassroots level and its capacity to resist the state-sponsored project.

Now, this area falls under the jurisdiction of the newly created Bodoland Territorial Autonomous District (BTAD). This has happened as a consequence of the long-drawn-out Bodoland movement for tribal autonomy which succeeded in gaining some autonomy for the Bodo tribals under certain provisions of the Indian constitution. Here, political structure and the arrangements are somewhat more decentralized and autonomous compared to the non-tribal areas of Assam. Hence, it is difficult for the centre and the state (the Delhi-Guwahati nexus) to impose their dictates at will. These political factors also helped the resistance movement to successfully resist the implementation of the PDP. However, the all-powerful state and its agency, the Brahmaputra Board, have not remained inactive. They made all kinds of efforts to weaken the resistance movement on one hand, and resorted to coercive measures in order to start implementing the project at hand, on the other.

The potential displacees as a part of their resistance movement, protest and demand, planned a peaceful *Dharna* at the state capital complex Dispur within the city of Guwahati on 29th October 2002. Thousands of villagers came to Guwahati to register their protest and demand the scrapping of the PDP. On their way to Dispur, they were stopped at Amingaon, the western outskirt of the city at a distance of more than 20 kilometres from the state capital complex. The protesters were determined to come to Dispur and the police were determined to stop them from entering the city by any means. The police resorted to *lathicharge* and used tear gas to stop the people from going to Dispur. A large number of people including women and children were injured in the police action and consequently, many of them were hospitalized. The movement considered this as an undemocratic and repressive act of the state.

However, though the police stopped a large number of protesters through blatantly coercive means from entering the capital complex, yet a large group of people gathered at the Last Gate of the capital and demonstrated against the PDP on the same day, that is, 29th October 2002. Those who joined the demonstration included the activists of the influential All Bodo Students' Union (ABSU), MPs and MLAs belonging to the Bodoland Demand Legislative Party (BDLP), All Rabha Students' Union (ARSU) and the All Bodo Employees' Federation (ABEF). The media persons in Guwahati covered this demonstration prominently. The police allowed the tribal elite leaders to register their solidarity with the resistance movement and to protest against the PDP, but barred the grassroots non-elite leaders and their supporters from joining the demonstration at the state capital.

Repressive measures and threat of repression continued for a long time. On 17th September 2002, when some young people were engaged in wall-postering against the construction of model houses for resettlement built by the Brahmaputra Board near the project site; the police resorted to selected target firing. The use of brute force by the state angered the people very deeply. They were protesting because they were convinced that the Brahmaputra Board officials were involved in corruption in coalition with contractors and politicians. As per the package, the Board spent Rs 12,462 in the construction of each model house. However, the people believed that the kind of house the Board was building would never cost more than Rs 3,000. According to them, the Board officials inflated the cost to more than four times the actual cost. The people could not accept the kind of small and absolutely low quality houses that the Brahmaputra Board wanted to offer them in their R&R package. From my field visit, I found that the houses of even the poorest sections of the people in the proposed project area were far better than the model R&R house in terms of quality and bigger in terms of size. The people said that such houses were absolutely inadequate to accommodate even a small family properly; and they would not accept such an R&R package.

However, the biggest protest action against the PDP took place on 29th January 2004 and continued upto 4th March 2004 for 35 days without any interruption. On 29th January 2004, a big contingent of officials from the district administration and the Brahmaputra Board arrived at Thalkuchi, the proposed site of the project, in order to do the land survey and to assess the compensation requirements of the people. They also set up a big camp to accommodate the officials and the staff of the revenue department for the purpose. They were also backed up by a large police contingent. This created a situation of confrontation; between the government bent on going ahead with the project and the people determined to resist the project.

The leadership of the resistance movement had been organizing all the people living in the proposed project-affected areas through their organizational network and had established links with each and every household. Realizing the danger coming their way, all the villagers came out from their homes and blocked all the roads, barring the officials from entry into the villages in order to stop the survey work. Almost 6,000 families and about 40,000 to 50,000 people joined the protest and blocked the entry of the officials. Significantly, half of the protesters were women. The old and the children too joined the protest *en masse* to stop the survey. The government officials first tried to convince the people to allow them to do the work assigned by the government. When they failed to do so, they threatened the people with dire consequences if they continued to block the official work of the government. The people refused to listen to the government officials' order to remove the blockade. On the next day, 30th January 2004, the police resorted to blank firing to scare them away and detained a few leaders of the movement in the camp and tried to transport them to the district headquarters at Nalbari in a police vehicle. People stopped the vehicle from moving and pressurized the police into releasing them all. The impasse continued for days together—no one was in a mood to give up.

At last, the officials attempted to do the survey of a few families to which the people did not agree. Ultimately, the government officials and the police had to go back without completing the assigned task of the state after 35 long days of face to face confrontation with the people. This was a landmark success of the popular resistance movement against the state-sponsored development-induced displacement. This gave a tremendous boost to the morale of the people who had been fighting for a long time to stop the PDP.

During our field visit, the potential displacees told us that the Brahmaputra Board had indulged in floating two Non-governmental Organizations (NGOs) in the affected areas to mobilize the support of the people in favour of the construction of the PDP. The name of these two NGOs are according to the people—Assam Council for People's Action and *Manab Seva Sangh*. Under the initiative of these organizations, a meeting was held at Guwahati in August 2002 between the Brahmaputra Board and the members of the NGOs. In the same meeting, a co-ordination committee was formed for furthering co-operation of the people of the affected areas in constructing the dam. The leadership of the movement soon cautioned the people against such fake NGOs. Both the NGOs failed in their missions in the face of popular support against the construction of the dam.

The people of the affected areas are fighting vigorously against all the undemocratic moves of the government and they are determined not to leave their ancestral land and home at any cost. The people alleged that the press and the elite in Guwahati have not given adequate attention to their problems and protests. Only few papers in Guwahati covered the popular resistance and the events of 30th January 2004 and the so-called 'national press' remained totally silent on the event. Hence, the voice of the subalterns did not reach much beyond their small and peripheral territory. To hear the voice of such subalterns one needs to have a pair of very sensitive ears. The people lamented that those who run the country from the state capital, Dispur, and national capital, Delhi, do not hear the voices of the people living at an interior as well as a frontier area located near the Indo-Bhutan border. Centralization of the decision-making process has blocked its access to the voice of the subalterns living at the margins of the society and geography.

However, the formation of the Bodoland Territorial Council (henceforth BTC) has significantly transformed the equation between the state and the people's movement. The autonomy granted to the Bodos has given some cushioning effects to the encounter between the state and the movement. This is a positive step in making the polity gradually more decentralized. All the 38 villages of the affected area fall under the jurisdiction of the newly constituted BTC. And for implementing any developmental project the consent of the BTC is a must now. As a result, the state and the central government are unlikely to succeed in implementing any state-sponsored developmental projects including the PDP without the consent of the BTC. As the majority of the people living in the area are Bodos, it is essential for the BTC/Bodo leadership to remain sensitive to the needs and aspirations of the people in general and the needs of the Bodos in particular. Because of this factor, the state may find it extremely difficult to go ahead with the PDP. Now the people of the area have realized the importance of political decentralization for the people living at the margins of the society. This is likely to act as an inclusionary political process ensuring popular participation at the grassroots level and empowering the disempowered people. The resistance of the subalterns has strongly interrogated the post-colonial development paradigm and its regime from a location far away from the centre of power. The response of the state to the interrogation will to a large extent determine the nature and future of the movement that is struggling for the last 37 years for a democratic, dignified and human space within a larger political society. Now the resistance movement is somewhat dormant, the state too is silent. However, for the threatened people the movement continues to exist and for the state the project is still in hand. All this does not reflect the end of the long-standing contestation. The state is again trying to revive the PDP. It is still very much a part of the state agenda. It seems that the state is exploring an alternative route which avoids confrontation with the threatened people by shifting the location of the water reservoir further upstream of the river, that is, very close to India-Bhutan border. This is likely to help in reducing the quantum of displacement of the population and at the same time avoiding the submergence of prime agricultural land. The Assam government, the Brahmaputra Board and the contractors: all want this project to be implemented. They find it absolutely unreasonable not to utilize the fund that the Government of India has offered for the commissioning of the PDP. Very significantly, the Bodoland People's Political Front (BPPF) which was vehemently opposed to the project in the past, is now a partner of the Congress led coalition government in Assam since 2006. Their role is going to be crucial in commissioning or abandoning the PDP. At the present juncture, they are not in a position to decide whether to go with the state government or to go with the threatened people who voted for them decisively to be a part of the state government in the elections of 2006 to the state legislature.

D. Beyond Siang, Subansiri, Tipaimukh and Pagladiya etc: The Incomplete Dossier

It is not that the people are apprehensive about the mega hydroelectric projects under construction; they are also dissatisfied with the completed ones. Negative effects of these projects have become very obvious to them notwithstanding what proponents of the dams have been saying. For example, the Umium Hydroelectric Projects located just 16 kilometres away from Meghalaya's capital town Shillong, was constructed by the Assam State Electricity Board in mid-sixties of the last century. However, consequent upon reorganization of Assam in 1972, this project was transferred to the Meghalaya State Electricity Board. This project now generates power far below its original stipulation. Siltation has reduced the capacity of the water reservoir very significantly. It has even failed to adequately meet the power requirement of Shillong. Similar is the case with the Loktak Hydroelectric Project near Manipur's capital town Imphal. The Tripura experience is also very painful. The Dumbur Hydroelectric Project displaced about 40,000 tribal people from their prime agricultural land only to generate 8.6 megawatt power! Now it generates less than half of its targeted power. Voices have been raised to decommission the Dumbur project totally. As an alternative, it has been suggested to go in for a large gas-based thermal power project so as to use the hitherto unused natural gas found in Tripura. This can meet not only the entire power demand of the state of Tripura, but it would be able to sell its surplus power to the neighbouring North Eastern states and Bangladesh also.

The recently completed Ranganadi Hydroelectic Project under the NEEPCO located in Arunachal Pradesh, too, has proved highly defective. It has failed to generate the targeted amount of power. The project diverted the river Ranganadi through a 9 kilometre long tunnel to the river Dikrong. Consequently, the quantum of water in the river Dikrong has increased substantially inducing heavy floods in the downstream areas of Lakhimpur district regularly. On the other hand, the river Ranganadi which is the lifeline of many people including the Mishing tribal of Lakhimpur district has virtually dried up as a result of the artificial diversion. Rivers Ranganadi and Subansiri, both have been the part and parcel of the culture, civilization and memories of the Mishing tribal in Lakhimpur and Dhemaji districts. The diversion of Ranganadi has affected the community life of the Mishings very significantly. They are also apprehensive of their future because the ongoing LSP and the proposed Middle Subansiri and Upper Subansiri projects in the upstream of the river in Arunachal Pradesh are also likely to affect the natural flow of the river Subansiri. People living in the upstream of the river in Arunachal Pradesh are, of course, no less apprehensive than their brethren downstream. They feel that the threat of mega dams is common to all of them and they must fight it back together.

The Karbi-Langpi Hydroelectric Project is located in a tribal area in the hilly Karbi-Anglong District in Assam which is under construction since 1979. More than a quarter century has passed; the cost has accelerated highly; and it has become a big burden on the Government of Assam and its people. In the eyes of the public, the Karbi-Langpi project has become a symbol of corruption and inefficiency of the Assam State Electricity Board. Accountability, transparency, efficiency and honesty have all been placed in cold storage.

E. Across the International Border...

A very significant event took place in the national capital, New Delhi on 28th June 2005. Hundreds of Myanmar refugees living in India, under the banner of Anti-Tamanthi Dam Campaign Committee (ATDCC), demonstrated against the construction of 1,200 megawatt hydroelectric project in the Kuki tribal dominated areas of Myanmar adjoining Manipur in India's eastern border. Significantly, the project is being constructed with the help of India's NHPC. The protesters submitted a memorandum to the Prime Minister of India and others pointed out that the project would displace 3,600 Kuki tribals from 35 villages and submerge about 1,700 acres of agricultural land. The Kukis are a small tribal community but the mega dam would affect them in a big way, directly attacking and snatching away their land, livelihood, culture and community life. It needs to be kept in mind that consequent upon the arbitrary drawing of the colonial political map and keeping it intact during the post-colonial period made many Kukis and Nagas a transnational community. Some of them have been living in Myanmar across the Indian border.

The ATDCC appealed to the Government of India to stop funding and providing manpower and technical know-how to the Tamanthi Hydroelectric Project which would 'in no way benefit the local Kuki people' (for details see Staff Correspondent, *The Hindu* 2005). In their memorandum to the Government of India, they urged upon to stop all forms of investment in Myanmar until genuine democracy was restored, as the investment was strengthening the military dictatorship and supporting its strategy to subjugate the indigenous people (ibid.). The memorandum also pointed out that as the dam site is located in the largest national park in Myanmar, the submergence would threaten the habitat of many endangered wild species including rhinos, tigers, leopards, Asian golden cats, gorillas and hornbills.

Grassroots Resistance, Civil Society Initiatives and Networking

Consequent upon the decision of the centre to go in for a huge number of large reservoir based hydroelectric projects in North East India, a large number of civil society organizations and the NGOs etc. became very active in raising questions about the ongoing as well as the proposed projects. They tried to link the question of dams with the question of development of North East. Two regional consultations were held on Dams and Development; first at Mawlein in Meghalaya in July 2001 organized by the CCDD, Manipur and second at Siliguri in April 2002 organized by NESPON. In these consultations, all the participants collectively raised some very fundamental questions concerning the dams in North East India, that is (see Menon 2005: 30).

1. Have the development needs and objectives been formulated through an open and participatory process at local and regional level?

2. Has a comprehensive option assessment for water and energy resource development been done?
3. Have the social and environmental factors been given the same significance as techno-economic aspects in assessing options?
4. Do we have a basin-wide understanding of the ecology of rivers and the dependence of local communities on them?

The state has not answered these crucial life and death questions involving the people of North East. For the state it has become difficult to answer these questions. It seems the state is seceding from the reality of facing such hard and real questions. In the process, the development has excluded the people. Now the excluded people want to be included in the development process. Here lies the conflict and contestation.

Grassroots resistance against displacement of population has increased gradually in the entire North East. They have also started interrogating the entire development paradigm of the post-colonial Indian state. They are slowly emerging as a significant political force in the North East outside the conventional power/electoral politics. This obviously signals to a qualitative shift in politics and political participation of the people. Various civil society organizations like environmental groups, rights groups, a part of the academia and the press have demonstrated some interest in the development issues and concern for the marginalized people. They are also trying to link their resistance movement with resistance movements of the people in similar situations. Solidarity of grassroots movements within the region and with the rest of India is gradually taking place though it is still at an embryonic stage. Once it takes off, it would help in empowering the disempowered marginalized groups and deepening of democracy in the mainland as well as in peripheral India. The unity and solidarity of the marginalized is crucial for deepening Indian democracy, protection of human rights and ensuring their own interest in a situation of socio-economic and political inequality.

One may also look at resistance movement,

as a response to the often appallingly bad consultation, baseline research, planning and implementation of resettlement projects and highlights serious shortcomings in the thinking behind such projects (Oliver-Smith 2002: 12). At a deeper level, resistance signifies that development itself has become a contested domain, an argument involving many voices and perspectives…. Resistance may be seen as a part of a discourse about rights … (ibid.).

Resistance also brings to the fore the question of people's right to self-determination and autonomy in the realm of development. It attempts to redefine the relationship between the state and its citizens, between mainland India and its troubled periphery.

Various civil society groups from the North East and a few from the rest of India organized a seminar on 'Assam's Flood Problem and Big Dams' under the auspices of the Lakhimpur-Dhemaji-Majuli Unnayon Sangram Samity held in early April 2005 and called for a public hearing on the Lower Subansiri Hydroelectric Project before the state government signed the MoU with the NHPC. It urged the Government of India to shelve its plan of turning North East India into the country's 'powerhouse' (*The Assam Tribune*. 6th April 2005: 1). The meet further observed:

Any move to construct large dams in the North East is fraught with grave danger in view of the region's seismic sensitiveness and perennial flood problems in Assam which is getting worse every year … there has been no proper study of the Lower Subansiri project's adverse downstream impact on the people as also the rich but fragile biodiversity of the area…. Environmental norms were blatantly flouted while clearing mega dams (ibid.).

Most of the dams in the pipeline in Arunachal Pradesh have no consideration for the downstream area. All rivers flow from Arunachal Pradesh down to Assam. Flood has been a major problem for the people of Assam's plains. There could have been some provisions for flood moderation through all the mega dams in Arunachal Pradesh but such provisions are absent. Now, it has been reported that dams located in Bhutan and Assam have added to the ferocity of flood in Assam in 2004 because of their panic discharge of water during high monsoons. In the massive 2006 Gujarat floods too, the dams instead of playing the role of moderators, played havoc as abettors (see Inter-Cultural Resources 2006).

The people of Majuli Sub-division of Jorhat, Lakhimpur and Dhemaji districts in Assam are feeling a deep sense of insecurity in the wake of ongoing construction of the LSP in the adjoining Arunachal Pradesh. If any accident takes place in the project as a result of faulty construction and/or earthquake, it is not only going to affect the people of Arunachal Pradesh but also the people of these three plains districts of Assam located downstream of the river Subansiri severely. The people in this area experienced the havoc of death and destruction in the wake of heavy flash flood induced by the great earthquake of 1950. If the LSP and the Siang dams were to burst, Lakhimpur and Dhemaji districts could be wiped out within a few hours. Bursting of any mega dam in Kameng district of Arunachal Pradesh can wipe out the entire Darrang and Baska districts of Assam. Dams being constructed in Arunachal Pradesh can severly affect the entire northern bank of the river Brahmaputra in the downstream.

While people in the downstream of the LSP in Assam are fighting a grim battle against the dams being constructed in the upstream outside their state, that is, in Arunachal Pradesh, the Government of Assam has not responded to the apprehensions and fear of its own people. It has largely remained silent. In recent times, very significantly, the powerful AASU has raised its concern and organized protest actions against the LSP. It seems the silence of the Assam Government is a deliberate and well-calculated action. It has seen how the Government of Arunachal Pradesh, which at one stage opposed the large reservoir based dam projects and went up to the Supreme Court of India in order to stop the construction of such dams, had to ultimately retreat from its anti-dam position. In a total turnaround of events, as stated earlier, it had to sign MoUs for constructing several mega dams. It would be reasonable to assume that the state governments have virtually no voice at all whatsoever before the central government on the centrally-sponsored development projects. The state governments are tacitly coerced by the central government to toe its line on development issues. It seems the Government of Assam has amply demonstrated more wisdom than its Arunachal Pradesh counterpart in not opposing the mega dam projects knowing very well its precarious position in the asymmetric relationship within the cosmetic Indian federalism! The role of the state government is, by and large, limited only to acquisition of necessary land for all the development projects. It needs to be pointed out that all the rivers from Arunachal Pradesh flow through the Brahmaputra valley and hence all the rivers are common resource for both the states. Any interference in the common river system in either of the states is likely to affect both the states simultaneously. Hence, there should have been consensus between both the Government of Arunachal Pradesh and Assam on the issue of construction of mega dams in the upstreams of the common rivers.

Earlier, we have seen the brutality of development in North East India, through our study of the Assam situation. In the name of development the state snatched land and livelihood from a large section of people. Most of them were marginalized and tribal people. The process of land acquisition by the state displaces people not only physically from their land, but also from their shelter, livelihood and community life. In the process, they have been experiencing a series of unending insecurities inseparably linked with their displacement. Obviously, the state has taken land 'in the public interest' from the ordinary masses and a large number of them, as elsewhere in India, are the tribal people. Instead of empowering the ordinary citizens, the state has disempowered them to a large extent. The people have largely failed to resist such kind of developmental aggression. The entire political space during the post-colonial period was occupied by the politics of ethnic identity which failed to articulate the question of development and empowerment of masses. However, with the dawn of 21st century the situation has drastically transformed. The people have started challenging the ongoing brutality of development and interrogating the state and its given development paradigm. Recent state-sponsored development efforts have been questioned by the ordinary people and not the elites of conventional politics. Response to mega dam projects aimed at converting the North East into India's powerhouse has been encountering stiff resistance from the threatened people. From Subansiri in Arunachal Pradesh and Tipaimukh in Manipur to Pagladiya in Assam, all these projects are being questioned collectively by the ordinary citizens. They have not only raised the question of population displacement, but also questioned the ecological sustainability, impact on the land downstream and on the rich biodiversity. They have been demanding the inclusion of human rights, dignity and justice besides popular grassroots participation in the planning and implementation of development agenda. All these popular resistances have taken the shape of New Social Movements. Of course, admittedly, these movements have not been fully organized. Some fluidity still exists. But they have shown the character of New Social Movements. Once they succeed in building solid local, regional, national and global network, they are likely to determine the popular politics decisively. Consequently, they will influence the politics of the North East and the rest of India. One can perhaps hope that the popular politics of New Social Movements will eventually lead to de-ethnicization of politics of identity in the North East. Mobilization for such movements is likely to bring to the fore the issue of survival and livelihood, human rights, community rights, environmental issues, questions of justice and popular participation in the development discourse. It seems that grassroots politics is slowly and steadily taking roots in the North East.

5

Conclusion

New Politics of Development: Interface between the State and the People

This study is an attempt at understanding the largely invisible process of development-induced displacement of population in an under-developed and peripheral region of India, that is, North East India during the post-colonial period. Notwithstanding state-sponsored development initiatives, the region remains one of the highly under-developed, ethnically sensitive and politically disturbed regions of India. Various development projects initiated by the state induced massive internal displacement of population in the region. This has virtually gone unnoticed, unattended and unaddressed. A large chunk of them have even gone undocumented. With the help of empirical data, this study has demonstrated the massive displacement of population in the North Eastern state of Assam induced by the state-sponsored development projects during the post-colonial period. This has affected mostly the weaker sections of society. In the name of development the state snatched land and livelihood from a large section of people, mostly marginalized and tribal. The process of land acquisition by the state displaces people not only physically from their land, but also from their livelihood, culture and community life. In the process, they have been experiencing a series of unending insecurities inseparably linked with their displacement. Obviously, the state has taken land 'in the public interest' from the ordinary masses and a large number of them, as elsewhere in India, are the tribal people. Instead of empowering the ordinary citizens living in the peripheral region through its development projects, the state has disempowered them to a large extent. They have been marginalized further by the development process. With the globalization of economy and its resultant primacy for the private capital and market, the people are being increasingly relegated to the background position. Their position is likely to worsen further in the absence of intervention of the state, civil society and the people.

The post-colonial Indian state, very paradoxically, taking advantage of the Land Acquisition Act 1894 introduced by its colonial predecessors, has been engaged in massive acquisition of land for various development projects. The LAQ, very often imposed 'in the public interest', has harmed the interest of the humble public. This piece of colonial law aimed at protecting and consolidating the interest of the colonizers in the Indian subcontinent, has been giving the one-sided absolute right to the post-colonial state at the cost of the rights of its own citizens. The sooner this LAQ is abrogated, the better it is for the marginalized people. The state now needs to rethink its land acquisition policy with a moral compass that adequately cares for justice and rights of the people. As we have already mentioned, India does not have a clear-cut resettlement and rehabilitation policy for the displaced people. It is high time that India not only goes in for a right-based democratic and empowering resettlement and rehabilitation policy for the people displaced by various development projects; but it also needs to go in for a right-based law simultaneously in order to protect the interest of the displaced people. Displaced persons instead of experiencing impoverishment in the post-displacement situation must experience empowerment. Benefit to the displaced persons should be an inseparable part of the development project. This is possible only when the potential displaced persons become an integral part of the development and its decision-making process. Now it is overdue to write the obituary for the redundant land acquisition policy and the top-down development policy simultaneously. However, most political parties including the left formations are not yet adequately prepared for such qualitative change. Consequently, in the absence of adequate response from the political parties to a political issue of such crucial importance for the marginalized people, one can see the emergence of popular struggles outside the conventional political party system in various parts of India, including North East India.

The people have largely failed to resist the brutality of development initiated by the all-powerful state. Development paradigm pursued vigorously by the post-colonial Indian state has been essentially colonial in character and consequences. Hence, it is capable of perpetuating brutality and indignity on a large section of its citizens. Of course, it benefits a smaller section. The whole post-colonial discourse has been a way of perceiving the world, it is a form of knowledge. It is a discourse that does not reflect reality but it reflects the crafty construction of reality. Thus, it insulates itself from alternative ways of thinking. The way out from such development lies in rejecting it and developing an alternative to such a development paradigm. The entire post-colonial political space in North East India was by and large occupied by the politics of ethnic identity which failed to articulate the question of development and empowerment of the masses. However, with the dawn of 21st century the situation has drastically changed. The common people have started challenging the ongoing brutality of development and interrogating the state and its given development paradigm. They want to prevent the brutality caused by state-sponsored development projects. The post-colonial agenda of state-sponsored development has remained largely centralized and somewhat regimented in nature and has failed to meet the developmental target of the state as well as the aspirations of the people. The failure on the part of the state in understanding the North East and its people trapped the region in the vicious cycle of underdevelopment and unrest. Experience of development has been painful to a large number of people living at the margins of history, society, economy and polity. Development process instead of becoming a process of inclusion, became a process of exclusion. It excluded a large number of people. In the process, the distance between the Indian state and its citizens living in the periphery remained problematic.

In the recent past, the Government of India has become visibly concerned, of course within the neo-liberal framework, about the imperative to develop the North East. This was reflected in approving and funding about 168 mega dams in North East. The state should have taken the concerned people into confidence before going in for such a huge number of dams, most of which are mega dams, in an ecologically fragile region. In view of mounting criticism against the constructions of mega dams both in India and all over the globe, the state should have gone in for a serious introspection and an objective review of the whole gamut of questions involving dams and development. There are viable, eco-friendly, pro-people and money-saving alternatives to destructive mega dam projects that could be found in India's own post-colonial experience and experiments with mega dam projects. The Indian state constricted by its own neo-liberal framework failed to rethink its own development discourse.

However, response to mega dam projects aimed at converting the North East into India's powerhouse has been facing stiff resistance from the threatened people. From Subansiri in Arunachal Pradesh and Tipaimukh in Manipur to Pagladiya in Assam; all these projects are being questioned by the ordinary citizens. They have not only raised the question of population displacement, resettlement and rehabilitation, but also the question of ecological sustainability, impact on the downstream, impact on rich biodiversity. They have been demanding the inclusion of human rights, human dignity and justice besides popular grassroots participation in the planning and implementation of development agenda. All these popular resistances have taken the shape of New Social Movements. Of course, these movements have not been fully organized. But they have shown the characters of New Social Movements. Once they succeed in building solid local, regional, national and global network, they are likely to determine decisively the popular politics. Consequently, they will influence significantly the politics of the North East and India too. One can perhaps hope that the popular politics of New Social Movements will eventually lead to de-ethnicization of politics of identity in the North East. Mobilization for such movement is likely to bring to the fore the issue of survival and livelihood, human rights, community rights, environmental issue, the question of justice and popular participation in the development discourse. It seems that this kind of politics is slowly and steadily taking roots in the North East.

In an unprecedented political development, a state government virtually endorsed the voice of the people who were opposing the construction of mega dams. It is something unbelievable like the Gujarat and Madhya Pradesh governments supporting and endorsing the demands of the *Narmada Bachao Andolan*! The crucial support of the state government in addition to support given by innumerable civil society organizations in the region has substantially strengthened the anti-mega dam movements. Consequently, the popular voice transformed into a mandate for the state government. A state government for the first time contested the 'centrality of the centre' in the context of centrally-sponsored mega dam projects in the state. This is a very significant development for India's 'formal' federal polity. Centrality of the centre is being contested by popular movements from a peripheral region. The centre has very successfully co-opted the Arunachal Pradesh Government to accept its centralized development paradigm. At the present stage of political development, the states, particularly the smaller ones without any significant financial resources, have virtually no option than to toe the line of the centre keeping in view the present structure and quality of federalism in India. Dams have strengthened the capacity of the centre and have reduced the potential of the states. In the process, the dams have become the symbol of power of the Indian states in the North East. However, the people continue to contest the centrality of the centre from this peripheral region.

Emergence of popular resistance outside the conventional party system based on new political cleavages is strengthening the democratic consciousness of the people living in a peripheral region of the world's largest democracy and successfully interrogating the centralized post-colonial developmental paradigm of the Indian state. This has situated the issue of development with the issue of livelihood, environment, rights and dignity of the citizens in the popular politics of New Social Movements. Qualitatively, this is a significant shift in the politics of the region which has been dominated by excessive and obsessive ethnicity of bewildering varieties for a long period of time.

Bibliography

A Staff Reporter 2005 Arunachal Against Mega Hydel Project, *The Assam Tribune*, 30th June 2005.

Alvares, C. and Ramesh Billorey 1988 *Damming the Narmada: India's Greatest Planned Environmental Disaster*, Third World Network/APPEN, Penang, Malaysia.

Amar Asam 2001 Report of IIT–Guwahati, *Amar Asam* (An Assamese daily) Guwahati, 2nd March 2001.

Barooah, Kalyan 2005 Controversy Dogs Subansiri Project, *The Assam Tribune*, 23rd February 2005.

Baruah, P.C. 1999 *The Saga of Assam Oil*, Spectrum Publication, Guwahati.

Baruah, S. 1999 *India Against Itself: Assam and Politics of Nationality*, Oxford University Press, New Delhi.

———2005 *Durable Disorder: Understanding the Politics of Northeast India*, Oxford University Press, New Delhi.

Baruah, S.K. 2002 *Assam Year Book*, Jyoti Prakashan, Guwahati.

Baviskar, A. 1995 *In the Belly of the River*, Oxford University Press, New Delhi.

Bharali, G. 2004 Development-induced Displacement: The Struggles Behind, Unpublished paper presented at the international seminar on *Development and Displacement: Afro-Asian Perspective*, Department of Political Science, Osmania University, Hyderabad.

Bhattacharjee, D. 2003 Development Projects and Displacement: A Case Study of the Panchgram Unit of Hindustan Paper Corporation in Tanmoy Bhattacharjee ed. *Problems of Internally Displaced Persons in Assam with special Reference to Barak Valley*, Department of Political Science, Assam University, Silchar.

Bhaumik, Subir 2005 Tripura: Decommissioning of Gumti Hydroelectric Project Crucial for Conflict Resolution, Monirul Hussain ed. *Coming Out of Violence: Essays on Ethnicity, Conflict Resolution and Peace Process in North East India*, Regency Publications, New Delhi for Indian Council of Social Science Research-NERC, Shillong.

——— 2000 Negotiating Access: Northeast India, *Refugee Survey Quarterly*, vol. 19, No. 2, 2000.

——— 2007 Land Reclaim Dispute Over Drying Dam, *BBC News*, 3rd April 2007.

Bijoy, Purendu 2005 Kar Sarthat Subansiri Jalavidyut Prakalpa, *Asam Bani*, vol. 51, No. 10 and 11, 2nd September and 9th September 2005.

Bordoloi, B.N. ed. 1986 *Alienation of Tribal Land and Indebtedness*, Tribal Research Institute, Guwahati, Assam.

——— 1999 *Report on the Survey of Alienation of Tribal Land in Assam*, Assam Institute of Research for Tribal and Scheduled Castes, Guwahati.

Centre for Science & Environment 1982 *State of India's Environment: First Citizens Report*, CSE, New Delhi.

Cernea, Michael 2000 Risks, Safeguards, and Reconstruction: A Model for Population Displacement and Resettlement, *Economic and Political Weekly*, vol. XXXV, No. 41, 7th October 2000.

Chhakchhuak, Linda 2006 Arunachal Pradesh: Development or Destruction, *The Hindu Survey of the Environment 2006.*

Cohen, Roberta 2003 Sovereignty and Responsibility: The Guiding Principles on Internal Displacement, Public lecture hosted by the Calcutta Research Group and the Refugees Study Centre, Jadavpur University, Kolkata 5th December 2003 published in the *Report of the First CRG Winter Course on Forced Migration, 2003*, Mahanirvan Calcutta Research Group, Kolkata.

Dainik Agradoot 2006 Report on Lapetkate Gas Cracker Project in *Dainik Agradoot*, (An Asamiya daily), Guwahati, 30th July.

Deka, Arunjyoti 2002 *Smirity Grantha*, the 17 biannual conference of the Pagladiya Bandh Parkalpor Khatigrasta Alekar Sangram Samitee, Thalkuchi.

Deka, Jagadish 2004 *Smirity Grantha*, the 18 biannual conference of the Pagladiya Bandh Prakalpor Khatigrasta Alekar Sangram Samitee, Padma Anand Bazar.

Deputy Commissioner, Barpeta 1966 J File No. A/c 57/65–66. Embankment of Beki River Project Land Acquisition Branch, Barpeta, District Collectorate.

——— 1967 B File No. A/c 65/65–66 Embankment of Beki River Project, LAQ Office, District Collectorate.

——— 1968 J, File No. A/c 70/65–66 Embankment of Beki River Project, LAQ Office, District Collectorate.

——— 1969 O File No. A/c 21/68–69 Embankment of Beki River Project, LAQ Office, District Collectorate.

——— 1970 I File no. A/c 3/70–71, Brahmaputra Dyke Project, LAQ Office, District Collectorate.

——— 1973 I File no. A/c 14/72–73, Brahmaputra Dyke Project, LAQ Office, District Collectorate.

——— 1974 D File no. A/c 6/73–74, Brahmaputra Dyke Project, LAQ Office, District Collectorate.

——— 1975 D File no. A/c 6/74–75. Embankment of Bhelengi River Project, LAQ Office, District Collectorate.

——— 1976 B File no. A/c 68/75–76. Gajia Kadang Gajia Gobindapur PWD Road Project LAQ Office, District Collectorate.

——— 1981 B, File No. A/c 105/80–81. Pahumara Irrigation Project LAQ Office, District Collectorate.

——— 1981 O File no A/c 31/80–81, Brahmaputra Dyke Project LAQ Office, District Collectorate.

——— 1986 K File No. A/c 9/84–85, Brahmaputra Dyke Project LAQ Office, District Collectorate.

Deputy Commissioner, Bongaigaon, 1973 A File No. BLA7/2002. 2nd April 2002, Bongaigaon Refiney Petrochemicals Project, LAQ Office, District Collectorate.

Deputy Commissioner, Cachar 1948 A File No. LA-2/1948–49, dated NA, Land for Displaced Person, Silchar, LAQ Office, District Collectorate.

——— 1948 B File No. LA-11/1948–49, dated NA, Land for Displaced Persons, Silchar, LAQ Office, District Collectorate.

——— 1953 A File No. LA-11/53–54, dated NA, Land for Landless Persons, Silchar, LAQ Office, District Collectorate.

——— 1953 B File No. LA-1/53–54, dated NA, Project Officer Community Project, Silchar, LAQ Office, District Collectorate.

——— 1956 F File No. LAC-17/56–57, dated NA, K.B Road Lantigram, Silchar, LAQ Office, District Collectorate.

——— 1956 G File No. LAC-13/56–57, dated NA, K.B Road, Silchar, LAQ Office, District Collectorate.

Deputy Commissioner, Cachar 1966 A File No. LAC-26/66–67, dated NA, Dwarband Police Outpost, Silchar, LAQ Office, District Collectorate.

——— 1971 C File No. LAC-14/71–72, dated NA, Police Out Post at Rongpur, Silchar, LAQ Office, District Collectorate.

——— 1972 E File No. LAC-5/72–73, dated NA, Construction of Watch Post, Silchar, LAQ Office, District Collectorate.

——— 1976 C File No. LAC-6/76–77, dated NA, BSF Headquarters, Silchar, LAQ Office, District Collectorate.

——— 1976 F File No. LAC-1/76–77, dated NA, Post Office Fulertal, Silchar, LAQ Office, District Collectorate.

——— 1996 A File No. File No. LAC-6/96–97, dated NA, BSF Headquarters, Silchar, LAQ Office, District Collectorate.

Deputy Commissioner, Dibrugarh 1999 A File No. DRA 23/1999 dated 13th March 1999. Extension of Runway Approach Light System and Glide path of Dibrugarh, Airport LA Office Dibrugarh, District Collectorate.

Deputy Commissioner, Goalpara 1987 T File No. GRQ22/PT3/87, dated NA, B.G Railway Project LAQ Office, District Collectorate.

——— 1988 I File No. GRQ14/88, dated NA, B.G Railway Project LAQ Office, District Collectorate.

——— 1988 O File No. 16/88, dated NA, B.G Railway Project LAQ Office, District Collectorate.

——— 1989 A, File No. 85/89, dated NA, for Office Accommodation of Sericulture. LAQ Office, District Collectorate.

——— 1990 A File No. GRQ 24/91, dated NA, B.G Railway Project LAQ Office, District Collectorate.

——— 1990 B File No. GRQ 14/91, dated NA, B.G Railway Project LAQ Office, District Collectorate.

——— 1991 R File No. 33/91, dated NA, B.G Railway Project LAQ Office, District Collectorate.

——— 1992 A File No. 9/92, dated NA, B.G Railway Project LAQ Office, District Collectorate.

——— 1992 G File No. GRQ 5/92, dated NA, B.G Railway Project LAQ Office, District Collectorate.

Deputy Commissioner, Golaghat, 1969 I File No. S.G.Q 1/23/1969 dated. NA. National Highway 37 Project, Golaghat LAQ Branch.

——— 1980 D File No. L.A. Case no. 8/1980–81 dated. 6th December 1981. Bridge on N.H. 39 project. Golaghat LAQ Branch.

Deputy Commissioner, Hailakandi 1990 B File No. L.A. Case No. 2/90(J). District Jail Project, Hailakandi, L.A Branch District Collectorate.

Deputy Commissioner, Kamrup (Urban) 1963 A File No. LA Case No. 341/63 dated 22nd March 1963, N.H Bypass Project, LAQ Office, District Collectorate.

——— 1963 C File No. LA Case No. 7/70, dated 11th January, Defence Project, LAQ Office District Collectorate.

——— 1963 G File No. LA Case No. 308/63, dated NA, National Highway 37 Bypass Project, LAQ Office, District Collectorate.

——— 1963 N, File No. LA Case No. 281/63, dated NA, Guwahati Refinery Project, LAQ Office, District Collectorate.

Deputy Commissioner, Kamrup (Urban) 1964 A File no. LA Case No. xii A24/22/63, dated 2nd June 1964, Narengi Khanapara Military Road Project, LAQ Office, District Collectorate.

——— 1972 A, File no. LA Case No. 80/49, dated. 6th May 1972, Post Exchange Office, District Collectorate.

——— 1972 D, File no. LA Case No. 42/72, dated 13th June 1972, Embankment Muskata Project LAQ Office, District Collectorate.

——— 1975 A, File No. LA Case No. 42/75, dated 10th March 1975, Defence Project LAQ Office, District Collectorate.

——— 1981 C, File No. LA Case No. 26/81, dated 25th September1975, Defence Project LAQ Office, District Collectorate.

——— 1983 A File No. LA Case No. 5/83, dated NA BSF Headquarters Project LAQ Office, District Collectorate.

——— 1983 G File No. LA Case No. 5/83, dated 27th July 1983, Battalion Headquarters Project LAQ Office, District Collectorate.

——— 1984 A File No. LA Case No. 5/83, dated 7th March 1984 BSF Headquarters, LAQ Office, District Collectorate.

——— 1986 D File No. LA Case No. 5/85, dated 5th September 1986, Nursery Seeding Distributor Project, LAQ Office, District Collectorate.

——— 1986 H File No. LA Case No. 3/86, dated 2nd August 1986, Adabari Bus Stand Project LAQ Office, District Collectorate.

——— 1987 A File No. LA Case No. 5/87, dated 9th September 1987, A.G Office, LAQ Office, District Collectorate.

——— 1994 B File No. LA Case No. 5/94, dated 17th September 1994, Sonapur Weekly Market Project, LAQ Office, District Collectorate.

——— 1999 B, File No. LA Case No. 12/99, dated 18th November 1999, Defence (Air Force) Project, LAQ, Office, District Collectorate.

Deputy Commissioner, Kamrup (Rural) 1960 A File No. L.A. Case No. 92/61–62 dated. 28th November 1960, Embankment project, Guwahati, L.A Office, District Collectorate.

——— 1960 C File No. L.A. Case No. 51/61–62 dated N.A. Baralia River Embankment Guwahati, L.A Office, District Collectorate.

——— 1964 E File No. L.A. Case. No. 95/64–65 dated 31st January 1964. National Highway 31 Project, Guwahati, L.A Office, District Collectorate.

——— 1964 F File No. L.A. Case. No. 76/64–65 dated. 31st January 1960, Puthimari Embankment Project, L.A Office District Collectorate.

——— 1964 J File No. L.A. Case No. 84/64–65 dated.NA Pagladia Embankment Project, L.A Office Guwahati District Collectorate.

——— 1965 A File No. L.A Case No. 21/67–68 dated 14th July 1966, Guwahati Medical College Project L.A Office Guwahati District Collectorate.

Deputy Commissioner, Kamrup (Rural) 1972 E. File No. L.A. Case No. 114/72. Dated N.A. National Highway 31Project, Guwahati, LA Office, District Collectorate.

——— 1986 I File No. L.A. Case. 9/85. dated 28th February 1986, B.G Rly Line Project, Guwahati, LA Office, District Collectorate.

——— 1987 M File No. L.A. Case No. 29/87 dated 19th January 1987, Jogighopa-Guwahati B.G Rly, Guwahati, LA Office, District Collectorate.

——— 1988 I, File No. L.A. Case. No. 29/88. dated 22nd November 1988, B.G Rly Line Project, Guwahati, LA Office, District Collectorate.

Deputy Commissioner, Kamrup (Rural) 1988 L File No. L.A. Case No. 24/88. dated 11th October 1988, B.G Rly Line Project, Guwahati, LA Office, District Collectorate.

—— 1988 N File No. L.A. Case No. 20/88. dated 27th August 1988, B.G Rly Line Project, Guwahati, LA Office, District Collectorate.

—— 1988 O File No. L.A. Case No. 18/86. dated 27th February 1988, B.G Rly Line Project, Guwahati, LA Office, District Collectorate.

—— 1989 A File No. L.A. Case No. 41/88. dated 22nd December 1989, B.G Rly Line Project, Guwahati, LA Office, District Collectorate.

—— 1990 A File No. L.A. Case No. 23/64. dated 30th October 1990, National Highway Project, B.G Rly Line Project, Guwahati, LA Office, District Collectorate.

—— 1990 B File No. L.A. Case No. 10/90. dated 8th February 1990, Embankment Project, B.G Rly Line Project, Guwahati, LA Office, District Collectorate.

—— 1995 G File No. L.A. Case No. 14/92. dated 14th November 1995, B.G Rly Line Project, Guwahati, LAQ Office, District Collectorate.

Deputy Commissioner, Karbi Anglong 1976 E, File No. L.A.C1/76. dated 20th July 1976, Kapili Embankment, LAQ Office Diphu, District Collectorate.

—— 1984 A File No. LAC-3/84, dated 11th July 1984, NH 36, LAQ Office Diphu, District Collectorate.

—— 1984 C File No. LAC-3/84, dated 7th December 1984, NH 36, LAQ Office Diphu, District Collectorate.

—— 1986 D File No. LAC-1/86, dated 23rd October 1986, NH 36, LAQ Office Diphu, District Collectorate.

—— 1986 I File No. LAC-2/86, dated 25th July 1986, Dighalpani Irrigation, LAQ Office Diphu, District Collectorate.

Deputy Commissioner, Karimganj 1971 D File No. LAC-5/71–71. B.S.F. Headquarters Project, Karimganj L.A Branch, District Collectorate.

—— 1983 D File No. LAC-1/83–84. B.S.F. Headquarters Project, Karimganj L.A Branch, District Collectorate.

Deputy Commissioner, Lakhimpur 1961A File No. LA-14/61–62, dated 30th October 1961, Dikrong River Dyke Lakhimpur, LAQ Office, District Collectorate.

—— 1969 A File No. LA-100/60–70, dated 19th February 1970, Pabha River Embankment Lakhimpur, LAQ Office, District Collectorate.

—— 1969 B File No. LA-42/60–70, dated 20th January 1969, Dikrong River Embankment, Lakhimpur, LAQ Office, District Collectorate.

—— 1970 A File No. LA-15/70–71, dated 8th June 1971, Ranganadi Embankment LAQ Office, District Collectorate.

—— 1981 A File No. LA-3/81–82, dated 3rd September 1981, Dikrong River Embankment, Lakhimpur, LAQ Office, District Collectorate.

—— 1981 B File No. LA-2/81–82, dated 3rd September 1981, Dikrong River Embankment, Lakhimpur, LAQ Office, District Collectorate.

—— 1981 C File No. LA-1/81–82, dated 3rd September 1981, Dikrong River Embankment, Lakhimpur, LAQ Office, District Collectorate.

—— 1982 A File No. LA-8/82–83, dated 27th March 1982, K.B Road, Lakhimpur, LAQ Office, District Collectorate.

—— 1982 B File No. LA-5/82–83, dated 11th May 1982, Pichala River Irrigation, Lakhimpur LAQ Office, District Collectorate.

Deputy Commissioner, Lakhimpur 1983 A File No. LA-5/83–84, dated 31st March 1983, Subansiri Dyke Lakhimpur LAQ Office, District Collectorate.

—— 1983 B File No. LA-5/83–84, dated 26th May 1984, Ranganadi Embankment Lakhimpur LAQ Office, District Collectorate.

—— 1983 C File No. LA-18/83–84, dated 4th December 1984, Ranganadi Embankment Lakhimpur LAQ Office, District Collectorate.

—— 1983 D File No. LA-2/83–84, dated 3rd March 1984, Brahmaputra Dyke, Lakhimpur LAQ Office, District Collectorate.

—— 1983 E File No. LA-4/83–84, dated 6th September 1985, Brahmaputra Dyke, Lakhimpur LAQ Office, District Collectorate.

—— 1983 F File No. LA-1/83–84, dated 16th September 1985, Brahmaputra Dyke, Lakhimpur LAQ Office, District Collectorate.

—— 1983 G File No. LA-21/83–84, dated 18th July 1984, Ranganadi Embankment, Lakhimpur LAQ Office, District Collectorate.

—— 1983 H File No. LA-19/83–84, dated 12th September 1984, Ranganadi Embankment, Lakhimpur LAQ Office, District Collectorate.

—— 1983 I File No. LA-14/83–84, dated 2nd August 1984, Subansiri Dyke Lakhimpur LAQ Office, District Collectorate.

—— 1983 J File No. LA-24/83–84, dated 31st October 1984, Dikrong Irrigation Lakhimpur LAQ Office, District Collectorate.

—— 1983 K File No. LA-8/83–84, dated 7th October 1983, Subansiri Dyke Lakhimpur LAQ Office, District Collectorate.

—— 1983 L File No. LA-13/83–84, dated 2nd August 1984, Subansiri Dyke Lakhimpur LAQ Office, District Collectorate.

—— 1983 M File No. LA-12/83–84, dated 2nd August 1984, Subansiri Dyke Lakhimpur LAQ Office, District Collectorate.

—— 1983 N File No. LA-23/83–84, dated 31st October 1984, Borbali lift Irrigation Lakhimpur LAQ Office, District Collectorate.

—— 1983 P File No. LA-11/83–84, dated 2nd August 1984, Subansiri Embankment Lakhimpur LAQ Office, District Collectorate.

—— 1983 Q File No. LA-10/83–84, dated 2nd August 1984, Subansiri Dyke Lakhimpur LAQ Office, District Collectorate.

—— 1983 R File No. LA-17/83–84, dated 13th January 1984, Subansiri Embankment Lakhimpur LAQ Office, District Collectorate.

—— 1983 S File No. LA-7/83–84, dated 2nd August 1981, Subansiri Embankment Lakhimpur LAQ Office, District Collectorate.

—— 1983 T File No. LA-18/83–84, dated 5th January 1981, Rangnodi Embankment Lakhimpur LAQ Office, District Collectorate.

—— 1983 U File No. LA-3/83–84, dated 29th October 1985, Brahmaputra dyke Lakhimpur LAQ Office, District Collectorate.

—— 1983 V File No. LA-9/83–84, dated 9th August 1984, Subansiri Dyke Lakhimpur LAQ Office, District Collectorate.

—— 1983 W File No. LA-15/83–84, dated 2nd August 1984, Subansiri Dyke Lakhimpur LAQ Office, District Collectorate.

—— 1983 X File No. LA-2/83–84, dated 20th August 1983, Brahmaputra Dyke Lakhimpur LAQ Office, District Collectorate.

—— 1983 Y File No. LA-16/83–84, dated 22nd August 1984, Subansiri Dyke Lakhimpur LAQ Office, District Collectorate.

Deputy Commissioner, Lakhimpur 1985 A File No. LA-1/85–86, dated 19th November 1988, Dikrong Embankment Lakhimpur LAQ Office, District Collectorate.

—— 1985 B. File No. LA-9/85–86, dated 7th February 1986, Lilabari Deep Tubewell Lakhimpur LAQ Office, District Collectorate.

—— 1985 C File No. LA-8/85–86, dated 18th July 1987, Lilabari Deep Tubewell Lakhimpur LAQ Office, District Collectorate.

—— 1985 D File No. LA-10/85–86, dated 15th March 1986, Lilabari Deep Tubewell Lakhimpur LAQ Office, District Collectorate.

—— 1985 E File No. LA-7/85–86, dated 7th February 1986, Lilabari Deep Tubewell Lakhimpur LAQ Office, District Collectorate.

—— 1985 F File No. LA-6/85–86, dated 7th February 1986, Lilabari Deep Tubewell Lakhimpur LAQ Office, District Collectorate.

—— 1985 G File No. LA-11/85–86, dated 3rd October 1987, Dikrong Embankment Lakhimpur LAQ Office, District Collectorate.

—— 1985 H File No. LA-5/85–86, dated 30th April 1986, Pichala River Irrigation, Lakhimpur LAQ Office, District Collectorate.

—— 1986 A File No. LA-2/86–87, dated 31st July 1987, Sumdiri Embankment, Lakhimpur LAQ Office, District Collectorate.

—— 1993 A File No. LRA-III/28/93–94, dated 10th July 1996, Subansiri dyke Lakhimpur LAQ Office, District Collectorate.

—— 1993 B File No. LRA-III/25/93–94, dated 10th July 1996, Subansiri dyke Lakhimpur LAQ Office, District Collectorate.

—— 1996 A File No. LA-60/96–97, dated 2nd February 1999, Brahmaputra dyke Lakhimpur LAQ Office, District Collectorate.

—— 1996 B File No. LA-58/96–97, dated. 15th February 1999, Rangnodi Embankment Lakhimpur LAQ Office, District Collectorate.

—— 1997 A File No. LRA-59/97–98, dated 30th March 1999, Charikuria River Irrigation Lakhimpur LAQ Office, District Collectorate.

—— 1998 A File No. LA-1/98–99, dated 28th October 1998, Brahmaputra dyke Lakhimpur LAQ Office, District Collectorate.

—— 1998 B File No. LA-8/98–99, dated 9th March 1998, Brahmaputra dyke Lakhimpur LAQ Office, District Collectorate.

—— 1998 C File No. LA-3/98–99, dated 6th July 1999, Rangnadi Embankment Lakhimpur LAQ Office, District Collectorate.

—— 1998 D File No. LA-2/98–99, dated 9th March 1999, Brahmaputra Embankment Lakhimpur LAQ Office, District Collectorate.

—— 1999 A File No. LA-6/99–2000, Brahmaputra Dyke Lakhimpur LAQ Office, District Collectorate.

—— 1999 B File No. LA-5/99–2000, Brahmaputra Dyke Lakhimpur LAQ Office, District Collectorate.

—— 1999 C File No. LA-4/99–2000, dated 20th March Brahmaputra Dyke Lakhimpur LAQ Office, District Collectorate.

—— 1999 D File No. LA-3/99–2000, dated 13th October Brahmaputra Dyke Lakhimpur LAQ Office, District Collectorate.

Deputy Commissioner, Morigaon 1986 I File No. NRQ41/68. dated 13th March 1968, Kopili River Project LAQ Office, District Collectorate.

—— 1968 J File No. NRQ7/68. dated 9th February 1968, Kopili River Project LAQ Office, District Collectorate.

Deputy Commissioner, Morigaon 1968 K File No. NRQ41/68. dated 22nd March 1968, Kopili River Project LAQ Office, District Collectorate.
—— 1968 N File No. NRQ175/68. dated 9th January 1969, Dhing to Hiloikhunda B/ Dyke Project, LAQ Office, District Collectorate.
—— 1968 O File No. NRQ177/68. dated 18th June 1970, Dhing to Hiloikhunda B/ Dyke Project, LAQ Office, District Collectorate.
—— 1968 P File No. NRQ80/68. dated 30th April 1970, Dhing to Hiloikhunda B/Dyke Project, LAQ Office, District Collectorate.
—— 1969 G File No. NRQ46/69. dated 25th July 1969, Kopili Tributary Dyke Project, LAQ Office, District Collectorate.
—— 1969 H File No. NRQ66/69. dated 16th December 1969, Kopili Tributary Dyke Project, LAQ Office, District Collectorate.
—— 1970 G File No. NRQ44/70. dated 20th July 1970, Kalong Kopili River Dyke Project, LAQ Office, District Collectorate.
—— 1975 G File No. MRQ 12/75. dated 25th September 1975, Jagiroad Damgabari PWD rd Project, LAQ Office, District Collectorate.
—— 1975 H File No. MRQ 10/75. dated 25th September 1975, Jagiroad Damgabari PWD rd Project, LAQ Office, District Collectorate.
—— 1975 I File No. MRQ 10/75. dated 25th September 1975, Jagiroad Damgabari PWD rd Project, LAQ Office, District Collectorate.
—— 1975 P File No. MRQ 26/75. dated NA Kopili Tributary Dyke Project, LAQ Office, District Collectorate.
—— 1975 S File No. MRQ 15/75. dated 13th August 1969, Kopili Tributary Dyke Project, LAQ Office, District Collectorate.
—— 1976 H File No. MRQ 2/76. dated 24th July 1976 Kopili River Bridge Project, LAQ Office, District Collectorate.
—— 1976 J File No. MRQ 26/75. dated 17th February1981 Kopili Gobha Dioniara band Project, LAQ Office, District Collectorate.
—— 1976 K File No. MRQ 9/76. dated 17th February 1981 Kopili Gobha Dioniara band Project, LAQ Office, District Collectorate.
—— 1976 L File No. MRQ 8/76. dated 17th February 1981 Kopili Gobha Dioniara band Project, LAQ Office, District Collectorate.
—— 1976 M File No. MRQ 21/77. dated 17th February Kopili Gobha Dioniara band Project, LAQ Office, District Collectorate.
—— 1980 N File No. MRQ 27/81. dated 14th February 1985 Gobha Dioniara band Project, LAQ Office, District Collectorate.
—— 1982 A File No. LA 2/82. dated 4th May 1982 Bhuragaon Brahmaputra dyke Project, LAQ Office, District Collectorate.
—— 1982 B File No. LA 6/82. dated 26th April 1982 Bhuragaon Brahmaputra dyke Project, LAQ Office, District Collectorate.
—— 1982 C File No. MRQ 12/82. dated 27th May 1982 Bhuragaon Brahmaputra dyke Project, LAQ Office, District Collectorate.
—— 1985 A File No. MRQ 9/85. dated 26th July1985 Dhumkura Brahmaputra dyke Project, LAQ Office, District Collectorate.
Deputy Commissioner, Nalbari 1960 A File No. A/C 60/61–62, dated NA, Embankment on Pagladia Project LAQ Office, District Collectorate.
—— 1960 N File No. A/C 173/60–61, dated NA, Embankment on Pagladia Project LAQ Office, District Collectorate.

Deputy Commissioner, Nalbari 1965 H File No. A/C 43/64–65, dated NA, National Highway Project LAQ Office, District Collectorate.

—— 1968 L File No. A/C 27/67–68, dated NA, Brahmaputra Embankment Project LAQ Office, District Collectorate.

—— 1969 A File No. A/C 28/69, dated NA, Embankment on Pagladia Project LAQ Office, District Collectorate.

—— 1969 E File No. A/C 14/69, dated NA, Embankment on Pagladia Project LAQ Office, District Collectorate.

—— 1969 J File No. A/C 19/69, dated NA, Embankment on Pagladia Project LAQ Office, District Collectorate.

—— 1969 W File No. A/C 15/69, dated NA, Brahmaputra Embankment Project LAQ Office, District Collectorate.

—— 1969 X File No. A/C 81/66, dated NA, Brahmaputra Embankment Project LAQ Office, District Collectorate.

—— 1970 I File No. A/C 117/70, dated NA, Subankhati irrigation Project LAQ Office, District Collectorate.

—— 1970 R File No. A/C 102/70, dated NA, Sukla Irrigation Project LAQ Office, District Collectorate.

—— 1978 D File No. A/C 15/78–79, dated NA, Dist. Jail Nalbari Project LAQ Office, District Collectorate.

—— 1980 B File No. A/C 7/80, dated NA, Golding Flow Irrigation Project LAQ Office, District Collectorate.

Deputy Commissioner, Sonitpur, 1960 D File No. XII-31/60, dated 23rd May 1960, Defense purpose, Balisuti Bengali Gaon, Tezpur, LAQ Office District Collectorate.

—— 1961 C File No. XII-14/61, dated 16th January 1961, Vortak, Tezpur, LAQ Office District Collectorate.

—— 1961 D File No. XII-18/61, dated 18th February 1961, Vortak, Tezpur, LAQ Office District Collectorate.

—— 1961 E, File No. XII-16/61, dated 3rd May 1961, Vortak, Tezpur, LAQ Office District Collectorate.

—— 1962 A File No. XII-42/61, dated 28th March 1962, Vortak, Tezpur, LAQ Office District Collectorate.

—— 1964 C File No. XII-161, dated 7th May 1964, Defence purpose at Bebejia, Tezpur, LAQ Office, District Collectorate.

—— 1968 A File No. XII-43, dated 14th May 1968, Tezpur airfield, Tezpur, LAQ Office, District Collectorate.

—— 1969 C File No. XII-78, dated NA Defence purpose at Tubukijhar Tezpur, LAQ Office, District Collectorate.

—— 1970 A File No. 16/69-70, dated 15th October 1970, Airforce Project, Tezpur, LAQ Office, District Collectorate.

—— 1970 E File No. XII-77, dated 27th February 1970, Airforce Project, Tezpur, LAQ Office, District Collectorate.

—— 1979 B File No. XII-89, dated NA Defence cantonment atChariduar Tezpur, LAQ Office, District Collectorate.

Desai, Vandana and Potter, R.B. eds 2002 *The Companion to Development Studies*, Arnold, London.

Duarah, Ron 2006 Gas Cracker Project: Lapetkata People Seek Rehabilitaion Package, *The Assam Tribune*, Guwahati, 3rd August.

Dutta, Akhil Ranjan 2003 *Agony of the Tribals: A Case Study of Potential Displacees of the Pagladiya Dam Project in Assam*, A paper presented at the 14th Grassroots Politics Colloquium on Tribals and Displacement, Developing Countries Research Centre, University of Delhi, 14–15th February, Delhi.

Dwivedi, Ranjit 2002 Modules in Development-induced Displacement, *Development and Change*, vol. 33, No. 4, Blackwell Publishers.

Fernandes, Walter and Bharali, Gita 2006 *Development Induced Displacement and Deprivation in Assam 1947–2000: A Quantitative and Qualitative Study of Its Extent and Nature*, North Eastern Social Research Centre, Guwahati (unpublished Project Report)

Fernandes, Walter 2005 Blinkered Critics, *Down To Earth*, vol. 14, No. 3, 30th June 2005.

——— 2004 Dams and Displacement Woes, *The Statesman*, 15th July 2004.

Fisher, William F. 1999 Going Under: Indigenous People and the Struggle Against Big Dams: Introduction, *Cultural Survival* Quarterly, 23: 3, 29–32.

Gellert, Paul K and Lynch, Barbara D. 2003 Mega Projects As Displacement, *International Social Science Journal*, vol. LV, No. 1, UNESCO, March 2003.

Goswami, Dulal C. and Partha J. Das 2003 The Brahmaputra River in India, *The Ecologist Asia*, vol. 11, No. 1, January and March.

Government of Assam 1947–2000 *The Gazettes of Assam* from 1947 to 2000, Government of Assam.

——— 2003 *Statistical Hand Book of Assam 2003*, Directorate of Economics and Statistics, Guwahati.

——— 2004–05 *State Industrial Profile of Assam*, Director of Industries, Guwahati 2005 *CDs*. Director of Industries, Assam.

——— 2005 *CDs*, District Industries Centre, Karbi-Anglong District.

Government of India 2001 *Census of India 2001*, Series 1, Household Amenities and Assets.

——— 1961 *Census of India 1961, Assam.*

Guha, Amalendu 1980 Little Nationalism Turned Chauvinist: Assam's Anti-Foreigners' Upsurge, *Economic and Political Weekly*, Special Number, vol. XV, Nos. 41–43.

Hazarika, Anup 2005 *Bogibeel Dalang: Swapna aru Bastav* (in Assamese), *Prantik*, vol. XXIV, No. 19, 1–15th September 2005.

Hazarika, Sanjoy 1995 *Strangers of the Mist: Tales of War and Peace from India's North East*, Penguin Books, New Delhi.

Heijmans, Annalies, 2001 *Vulnerability: A Matter of Perception,* a paper presented at the International Workshop Conference 'Vulnerability in Distater Theory and Practice, 29–30th June 2001, Disasters Studies Programme, Rural Sociology Development Group, Wagenin-Gen University, the Netherlands.

Hussain, Monirul 1990 Nationality Question in North East India, *Seminar* (issue on the North East), No. 366, February.

——— 1993 *The Assam Movement: Class, Ideology and Identity*, Manak Publications, Delhi.

——— 1995 Refugees In the Face of Emerging Ethnicity in North East India, *Studies in Humanities and Social Science*, vol. 2, No. 2, 1995, Indian Institute of Advanced Study, Shimla.

——— 1999 Fear of Being Killed, Violated and Displaced: An Incomplete Dossier of Terrorism in Postcolonial Assam, in Kailash Agarwal ed. *Dynamics of Inter-group Relations in North East India,* Indian Institute of Advanced Study, Shimla.

——— 2000 State, Identity Movements and Internal Displacement in North East India, *Economic and Political Weekly*, vol. XXXV, No. 51, 15th December 2000.

——— 2002 State, Development and Population Displacement in North-East India, in C. Joshua Thomas ed. *Dimensions of Displaced People in North–East India*, Regency Publications, New Delhi.

Hussain, Monirul ed. 2005 A *Coming Out of Violence: Essays on Ethnicity, Conflict Resolution and Peace Process in North-East India*, Regency Publications, New Delhi for the Indian Council of Social Science Research, NERC-Shillong.

———— 2005 B North East India's Forgotten IDPs, *Forced Migration Review*, 24, Refugee Studies Centre, University of Oxford.

———— 2006 A Internally Displaced Persons in India's North East, *Economic and Political Weekly*, vol. XLI, No. 5, 4–10th February.

———— 2006 B IDPs in India's North East: Waiting for Elusive Resettlement and Rehabilitation, *Mainstream*, 12–18th May.

Hussain, Monirul and Phanjoubam 2007 *A Status Report on Displacement in Assam and Manipur*, Mahanirban Calcutta Research Group (CRG), Kolkata.

India Together 2006 *India Together*, 19th September 2006 (http://www.indiatogether.Org/photo/2004/eco-genhydro.htm.)

Intercultural Resources 2006 Press Release, *Big Dams Indicted for Flash Flood in Downstream*, New Delhi, 5th September 2006.

International Commission on Dams 1974 *Lessons from Dam Incidents*.

Iyer, V.R. Krishna 1998 'Marginalised Indian Humanity: Do the Bells of Constitution Toll for Them?' in Murli Desai etc. ed *Towards People-Centered Development*, Part I, Tata Institute of Social Sciences, Mumbai.

Kalin, Walter 2000 *Guiding Principles on Internal Displacement: Annotations*, The American Society for International Law and the Brookings Institution, Washington D.C.

Khagram, Sanjeev 2004 *Dams and Development: Transnational Struggle for Water and Power*, Oxford University Press, New Delhi.

Lianzela 2002 Internally Displaced Persons in Mizoram, in C. Joshua Thomas ed. *Dimensions of Displaced People in North East India*, Regency Publication, New Delhi.

Luthra, D.N. 1972 *Rehabilitation*, 25th Anniversary of Independence Series, Publications Division, Government of India, New Delhi.

Marks, Stephen P. 2004 'The Right to Development in Context' *in Centre* for Development and Human Rights, *The Right To Development: A Premier*, Sage Publications, New Delhi.

McCully, Patrick 1996 *Silenced Rivers: The Ecology and Politics of Large Dams*, International Rivers Network, USA.

———— 2002 Big Dams, Big Troubles, *New Internationalists*, March 2003.

Menon, Manju, Kanchi Kohli and Vogholikar, Neeraj 2003 The Northeast: Damming the Future, *The Hindu Survey of the Environment 2003*.

Menon, Manju, Vogholikar, Neeraj, Kanchi Kohli and Asish Fernandes 2003 Large Dams in the Northeast A Bright Future, *The Ecologist Asia*, vol. 11, No. 1, January–March 2003.

Menon, Meena 2005 A Myth Demystified, *The Hindu*, Sunday Magazine, 4th September 2005.

Misra, B.P. 1985 *The Assam Agreement and Its likely Fallout*, Citizens' Right Preservation Committee, Guwahati.

Misra, Udayon 1999 *The Periphery Strikes Back: Challenge to the Nation-state in Asssam and Nagaland*, Indian Institute of Advanced Study, Shimla.

Mohanty, Tapan R and Khan, Adil Hassan 2005 Dams of Division: Understanding the Baglihar Dispute, *Economic and Political Weekly*, vol. XL, No. 29, 16–22nd July.

Nag, Sajal 2002 *Contesting Marginality: Ethnicity, Insurgency and Sub-nationalism In North East India*, Manohar, New Delhi.

Nag, Sajal 2005 Land, Migrants, Hegemony: the Politics of Demography in North East India, in David R. Syiemlieh, Anuradha Dutta and Srinath Baruah ed. *Challenges of Development in North East India*, Regency Publications, New Delhi published on behalf of the Indian Council of Social Science Research—NERC, Shillong.

Narayanan, K.R. 2001 Let the Dams Not Ruin the Lives of Our Tribal Brothers and Sisters, *Mainstream*, vol. XXXIX, No. 11, 3rd March 2001.

N.H.R.C 2002 *National Human Rights Commission: Annual Report 2001–2002.*

Ojha, C.S.P and Singh V.P, 2004 Introduction, in Ojha C.S.P, Singh V.P and Sharma N ed. *The Brahmaputra Basin Water Resources*, Kluwer Acaemic Publishers, Dordrecht, The Netherlands.

Oliver-Smith, Anthony 2002 *Displacement, Resistance and the Critique of Development: from the Grassroots to the Global*, Final Report prepared for ESCOR R7644 and the Research Programme in Development Induced Displacement and Resettlement, Refugee Studies Centre, University of Oxford, (smaller version published in *Forced Migration Review*, No. 12)

Oommen, T.K. 2004 *Development Discourse: Issues and Concerns* Regency Publications, New Delhi.

Our Bureau 2006 Gas Cracker Project: Lepatkata Residents Demand Involvement in Land Survey, *The Assam Tribune*, 13th September 2006.

Our Correspondent 2006 Gas Cracker Project: 20 Hurt in Lepatkata Police Firing, *The Assam Tribune*, 8th September 2006.

Pamei, Aram 2001 Havoc on Tipaimukh High Dam Project, *Economic and Political Weekly*, vol. XXXVI, No. 13, 31st March–6th April 2001.

Patowary, Ajit 2006 Tipaimukh Hydel Project Faces People's Opposition, *The Assam Tribune*, 19th January.

Pattanaik, S.K, B.K. Das and Arthabandhu Das 1987 Hirakud Dam: Expectations and Realities, in PRIA ed. *People and Dams*, Society for Participatory Research in Asia, New Delhi.

Pegu, Suryadeep 2004 Subansiri Jalavidyut Prokalpor Prakitik Paribeshar Oparat Kuprabhav, *Prantik* (an Assamese fortnightly), vol. XXIII, No. 24, 16–30th November 2004.

Petterson, B 2002 A Development-induced Displacement in India, in Norwegian Refugee Council Global IDP project, *Internally Displaced People*, Earthscan, London and Sterling VA.

——— 2002 B Development-induced Displacement: Internal Affairs or International Human Rights Issue? *Forced Migration Review*, Issue No. 12.

Prabhu, Pradeep 1998 'Tribal Movements: Resistance To Resurgence' in Murli Desai, Anjali Monterio and Lata Narayan (eds.) *Towards People Centered Development*, Part I, Tata Institute of Social Sciences, Mumbai.

Prasad, Archana 2004 *Environmentalism and the Left*, Leftword, New Delhi.

P.R.O 2005 Public Relations Officer's Report, Nagaon Paper Mills, Jagiroad.

P.R.O 2005 Public Relation Officer's Report, National Textile Corporation Limited, Guwahati.

Ramachandran, Rajesh 2005 French Fry In A Hydel Soup, *Outlook,* 7th March 2005.

Ramanathan, Usha 1999 'Public Purpose: Points for Discussion' in Walter Fernandes ed. *Land Acquisition (Amendment) Bill 1998: For Liberalization Or for the Poor?* Indian Social Institute, New Delhi.

Rao, U. Bhaskar 1974 *The Story of Rehabilitation*, Publication Division, Government of India, New Delhi.

Rina, Togam 2005 Arunachal Sealed: Says No. To Reservoir Based Dams: Centre-state Clash Imminent, *Down To Earth*, vol. 14, No. 5, 31st July 2005.

Roy, Dunu 1994 Large Projects: For Whose Benefits? *Economic and Politcal Weekly*, vol. XXIX, No. 50.

———— 2000 *The Algebra of Infinite Justice*, Penguin Books, New Delhi.

Roy, Arundhati 1999 *The Greater Common Good*, India Book Distributors, Bombay.

Sagar, Ravi 2005 *Forest Rights of the Scheduled Tribes and Forest Dwellers: The Guwahati High Court Judgements and the Central Forest Bill*, North Eastern Social Research Centre, Guwahati.

Scudder, Thayer 2005 *The Future of Large Dams: Dealing with Social, Environmental, Institutional and Political Costs,* Earthscan, London.

Sengupta, Amit 2005 Eyeless in Yazali, *Tehelka*, vol. 2, issue 26, 2nd July 2005.

Sethi, Nitin 2005 Truth is More Slippery, *Down to Earth*, vol. 13, No. 24, 15th May.

Sinha, A.C. 1999 Tipaimukh Multi-purpose Project and the Recent Move for Its Completion, *Dialogue,* vol. 1, No. 1, October–December.

Special Correspondent 2005 President Alerts Nation on Need for Energy Independence, *The Hindu*, Delhi edition 15th August 2005.

Srivastava, S.C. 1979 *Migration in India*, paper No. 2, Ministry of Home Affairs, Government of India.

Staff Correspondent 2005 Myanmar Refugees Rally Against NHPC Plant, *The Hindu*, Delhi edition, 29th June 2005.

Staff Reporter 2005 Naamghar Destruction by NHPC Condemned, *The Assam Tribune,* 9th April 2005.

Subba, T.B 2003 One or Many Paths: Coping With Tibetan Refugees in India, In C.J. Thomas ed. *Dimensions of Displaced People in North East India*, Regency Publications, New Delhi.

Supreme Court of India 1982 *Lalchand Mahto & Others Vs. Coal India Limited*, Civil Original Jurisdiction MP No. 16331 of 1982, Supreme Court of India.

Talukdar, Sushanta 2005 Assam Opposes Expansion of NH 37, *The Hindu*, Delhi ed. 8th October.

Thakkar, Himanshu 2000 Large Dams: Disasters of Gigantism in Parasuraman S and Unnikrishnan Edition. *India Disasters Report: Towards A Policy Initiative*, Oxford University Press, New Delhi.

———— 2004 Diminishing Returns from Large Hydro Projects, *India Together*, in picture, September 2004.

———— 2006 Status of Large Dams, India: No. Lessons Learnt, *The Hindu Survey of Environment 2006*.

Thakuria, Nava 2004 Row Over A Dam, *Sahara Times*, 25th December 2004.

The Assam Tribune 2005 Tipaimukh Dam Construction Raises Bangla Concern, *The Assam Tribune*, Guwahati, 14th March, vol. 67, No. 71.

The Hindu 2006 *The Hindu Survey of Environment 2006*.

TOI News 2006 Power Ministry, Arunachal Government Pact Soon, *The Times of India*, Mumbai, 15th September 2006.

United Nations 1999 *Guiding Principles on Internal Displacement*, Office of the Co-ordination of Human Affairs, OCHA, United Nations.

Vandergeest, Peter 2003 Land To Some Tillers: Development Induced Displacement In Laos, *International Social Science Journal*, vol. LV, No. 1, UNESCO, March 2003.

Velath, Priyanca Mathur 2003 Refugees and IDPs: Are They Really So Destitute? Researching Internal Displacement: State of Art, Conference Reports, 7–8th February, Trondheim. Norway, *Forced Migration Review*.

World Bank 1994 *Resettlement and Development: Bank-wise Review of Projects Involving Involuntary Resettlement*, The World Bank, Washington D.C.

World Commission 2000 *Dams and Development: A New Framework for Decision* on Dams *Making, The Report of the World Commission on Dams*, Earthscan, London.

Websites

BBC News http://news.bbc.co.uk/go/pr/fr//2/hi/southasia/6509771.stm

NETV www.netvindia.com

North East Development and Finance Corp. www.database.nefdi.com

UNHCHR: http://www.unhcr.ch/development/approaches-04html.

World Commission on Dams http://www.dams.org

Index

About the Author

Monirul Hussain graduated from Cotton College, Guwahati and completed his MA from AMU, Aligarh. He did his M.Phil and doctoral research at the School of Social Sciences, Jawaharlal Nehru University, New Delhi and the post doctoral research at the University of Oxford. He was recipient of Commonwealth Fellowship in 1999 and South Asia Regional Fellowship (Senior) from the Social Science Research Council (SSRC), New York in 2004. He has contributed papers in national and international journals on society and politics in North East India. His book *The Assam Movement: Class, Ideology and Identity* (1993) received critical appreciations from far and wide. This book is regarded as an indispensable source for understanding Assam's colonial and post-colonial society and politics. He co-edited two volumes on *Religious Minorities in South Asia*: *Selected Essays on Postcolonial Situation* (2001) in addition to another volume entitled *Coming Out of Violence: Essays on Ethnicity, Conflict Resolution and Peace Process in North East India* (2005).

Professor Hussain had been a Visiting Fellow at the Queen Elizabeth House, University of Oxford and Visiting Professor at the School of Social Sciences, Jawaharlal Nehru University, New Delhi. Currently, he is Professor at the Department of Political Science, Gauhati University. Besides teaching at MA level and guiding research at doctoral level, he is now engaged in research on ethnicity, human security and forced migration in North East India.

Author's email:
monirulhussain@hotmail.com
guwahatimonirul@gmail.com